Reinspiring
The Corporation

Reinspiring
The Corporation

The Seven Seminal Paths to Corporate Greatness

Mark C. Scott

John Wiley & Sons, Ltd

Chichester · New York · Weinheim · Brisbane · Singapore · Toronto

Copyright © 2000 by John Wiley & Sons, Ltd.
         Baffins Lane, Chichester,
         West Sussex PO19 1UD, England

National   01243 779777
International   (+44) 1243 779777
e-mail (for orders and customer service enquiries):
cs-books@wiley.co.uk
Visit our Home Page on http://www.wiley.co.uk
                 or http://www.wiley.com

Other Wiley Editorial Offices

John Wiley & Sons, Inc., 605 Third Avenue,
New York, NY 10158-0012, USA

Wiley-VCH GmbH, Pappelallee 3,
D-69469 Weinheim, Germany

Jacaranda Wiley Ltd., 33 Park Road, Milton,
Queensland 4064, Australia

John Wiley & Sons (Asia) Pte Ltd. 2 Clementi Loop #02–01
Jin Xing Distripark, Singapore 129809

John Wiley & Sons (Canada) Ltd, 22 Worcester Road,
Rexdale, Ontario M9W 1L1, Canada

British Library Cataloguing in Publication Data
A catalogue record for this book is available from the British Library

Library of Congress Cataloging-in-Publication Data
Scott, Mark C.
   Reinspiring the corporation: the seven seminal paths to corporate
greatness / Mark C. Scott.
       p. cm.
   Includes bibliographical references and index.
   ISBN 0-471-86370-X (cloth)
   1. Industrial management.   2. Industrial organization.   I. Title.
HD31.S347 2000
658.4′063—dc21   99-059520

ISBN 0-471-86370-X

Typeset in Goudy 11/15 pt by Florence Production Ltd, Stoodleigh, Devon
Printed and bound in Great Britain by Biddles Ltd, Guildford and King's Lynn

This book is printed on acid-free paper responsibly manufactured from sustainable
forestry, in which at least two trees are planted for each one used for paper
production.

To Heather and our families

Contents

Preface

This book, although relatively compact, has matured over a long period of time, based on observations of companies that seem to be operating at considerably less than their full potential. This sort of unfulfilled torpor is commonplace but, like its human counterpart ME, hard to diagnose – indeed, the sceptical among us might claim, as many still do with ME, that it doesn't really exist. It is not obviously a failure of strategy, a notably poor financial performance or an excessively competitive market. It is – well – simply a lack of vigour, of will to grow, of enthusiasm; an absence of joy about the process of being in business.

Diagnosing that complaint and probing for the cure, the Amazonian violet, was where this book began. And it began several years ago before finding its way into the hands of a publisher. At the time the thesis it proposed seemed a little far-fetched or at least ahead of its time. But now its relevance is clear. Corporate ME has been acknowledged by enough serious thinkers and practitioners as a bona fide and endemic condition. We have all survived the prophesied Armageddon of Y2K. We sincerely believe now is the time to view business strategy afresh – to reinspire ourselves.

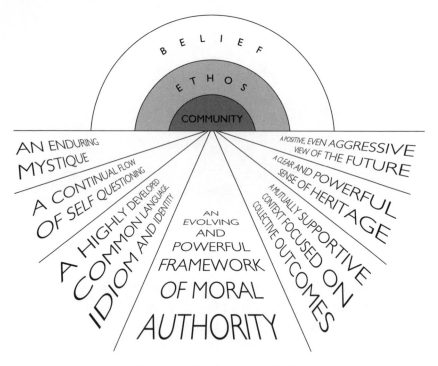

The reinspiration framework

Introduction:
the need for a new paradigm

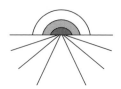

Most firms today have never faced a more competitive environment. The new millennium has dawned over a tough landscape. The past ten years have opened up all sectors to the cold wind of global competition. The unit cost of a basket of typical consumer goods has fallen 50 per cent in real terms. The average product life-cycle has halved. The last ten years have also seen a vastly increased focus on a single measure of competitiveness – share price.

These two forces – changes in the competitive environment and the ascendancy of shareholder value – have forced all businesses to adapt or die. The pressure to adapt, the quest for competitive advantage, has produced a period of unprecedented corporate re-invention and change. To be more exact, over the past decade the corporate world has been swept by seven major waves of re-invention – the tail end of the quality movement; downsizing; the core competencies regime and outsourcing; reengineering; the mergers and acquisition boom; the networked computerisation phenomenon; and empowerment. Although apparently very different on a superficial level, at heart these initiatives have all tended to focus on the denominator of the P&L – the cost side of the equation. The almost universal response to market changes has been the pursuit of greater cost efficiency.

The quality movement emerged with full force in the early 1980s in response to the push of Japanese multinationals into Western markets. Its principal focus was reducing scrap rates and enhancing process inefficiency, such as cycle and throughput time. Ten years on and the same mantle was then taken up by the reengineering movement which, championed by Hammer and Champy, sought to induce efficiency through a fundamental rethink of internal processes. A couple of years earlier, in response to the senior management scramble to fix flagging share prices in the late 1980s, the term 'downsizing' had been coined to describe a radical elimination of 'excess' capacity.[1] Downsizing, followed close on its heels by the core-competency regime, and then repackaged as reengineering, stripped an estimated $80 billion of 'non-core' costs from the Fortune 500 alone before it ran out of steam by the mid-1990s. Under the guise of outsourcing the process is, as we read, continuing apace. In 1998 outsourcing contracts were valued at $200 billion in the US market alone, with a 30 per cent rate of growth. That makes it probably the biggest transfer of assets in history.

Perhaps the single most obvious catalyst of asset elimination has been the merger and acquisition (M&A) process. The most readily available method of proving the value of a deal to shareholders has been the elimination of costs to boost combined margins. The M&A boom has grown relentlessly from annual deal value in 1995 of $500 billion to an estimated $2.6 trillion in 1999. And with it rationalisation and outsourcing have driven hard behind.

The biggest wave of re-invention has not, however, been the product of M&A activity. That honour is reserved for networked computing. Since the late 1980s, networked computing has been a fundamental underpinning of reengineering. It has also been a driver of the elimination of the middle management function. With the upsurgence of Intranets and Extranets, it has assumed a communicational as well as a financial control role.

---

[1] See Tomasko, Robert. *Downsizing: Reshaping the Corporation for the Future.* 1987.

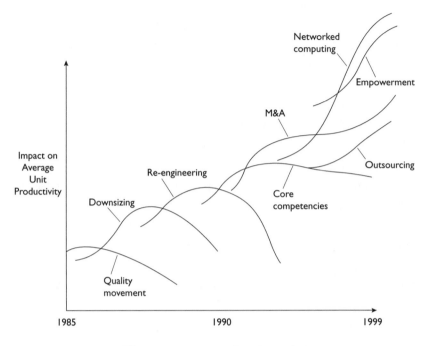

The seven waves of re-invention

It would be easy to mistake the phenomenon of networked computing as unrelated to the cost focused re-invention typhoon. It is, after all, closely linked to the empowerment process. In the wake of networked computing, the concept of empowerment in fact swept in for very practical reasons. Speedy management information flow and communication have meant that operating units can be given a modicum of operating independence while the financial reins are kept tight. That means the communicational and control role of middle management is no longer needed. The seven waves of re-invention are in fact all aspects of a single motion.

Is there anything wrong with this picture? On the face of it, the decade of efficiency has been a very successful one. Average unit costs of production have dropped some 40 per cent and productivity has risen 9 per cent annually on average over the decade. From 1990 to mid-1998 the Dow Jones and FTSE indexes rose at an average compound annual rate of over 17 per cent. Over the period collective shareholder wealth has more than doubled. That would not look like the harbinger of a problem. The institutional shareholder who bought stock in 1990 is a happy camper. Shareholder wealth creation has probably never been more rapid or expansive.

The trouble comes when you look at the sustainability of how it has been achieved. Don't forget, stock values are based on estimations of future, not historical, cash flows. For the past ten years the average large business has been altered out of all recognition. Bastions such as General Motors have shed at least 70 000 employees, AT&T 80 000, IBM 85 000. As quickly as they have been slimmed down, corporations have consolidated. From Asea and Brown Boveri through to Price Waterhouse and Coopers & Lybrand, the old names have been merged into reborn entities with global muscle. Virtually no sector has been untouched by major consolidation. The result? The driving down of fixed costs, combined with a mixture of bid premiums, enlarged market caps and rapid globalisation, has helped push up EPS and stock values to all time highs.

Clearly, the degree to which costs can be cut is finite; the number of sensibly priced and high-fit deals of a decent size is not unlimited. Yet, the cost-led and deal-led logic is a stubbornly prevalent imperative amongst management teams. The reason? Cost-led margin management is rewarded swiftly by the markets because its impact on profits is immediate. Post merger, stock values also tend to jump, sometimes dramatically as institutional interest is piqued. Organic growth combined with targeted fill-in acquisitions requires patience and investment. It takes time for revenue growth to turn to profit – like cultivating a fine garden. Unless you're into gardening, that's exasperating!

However, something is slowly dawning on most CEOs. Efficiency measures and non-organic growth do not have limitless potential in most sectors. It is now well established that as many as 75 per cent of large acquisitions and mergers in industrial and service sectors fail to deliver incremental shareholder value over the medium and long

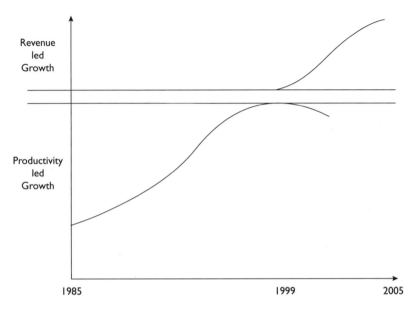

Revenue
led
Growth

Productivity
led
Growth

1985   1999   2005

The next wave: from productivity to revenue growth

term.[2] After all is said and done, the successful corporation has to be able to achieve sustainable and above average rates of organic growth, even if fill-in acquisitions continue to complement this process. There is an increasingly broad consensus that the next leg of the curve is dominantly an organic growth one, although consolidation will continue inexorably between firms that share similar core competencies.

Most firms are also now hitting the threshold of cost-led productivity gains. Competitive cost has become a hygiene factor rather than a source of differentiation. The question is beginning to shift to how to drive top-line growth in an environment where the only sustainable basis of competitive advantage is differentiation. This we will have much to say about presently.

---

[2] This is largely because they are not strategic in-fills which leverage existing assets and capabilities. Such in-fill acquisitions tend to be smaller, more laborious to execute and in this respect semi-organic.

The big question therefore is, what are the sources of sustainable differentiation for firms? The broad consensus is that the only real generic source of differentiation for Western companies is 'knowledge' – the collective intellectual assets of employees. In an age of readily available, cheap capital, where competitive costs are a hygiene factor, and which is characterised by a rapidly increasing service or 'brain' component, knowledge is the differentiator. You've heard it all before . . . and books on the subject abound.

The problem with knowledge for most businesses and their Boards is that it is intangible. It can be an extremely unnerving idea for firms used to the comfort of fixed assets, with clearly assignable balance sheet value and ownership, that their corporate value is invested in knowledge. Knowledge possesses neither of these characteristics. It is personalised. It tends to walk out of the building each night. It is also intensely tough to quantify or value as an accounting item.

The evolving knowledge management movement has tended to focus its energies on finding ways to allay these boardroom fears. On one hand, the bulk of energies have gone into 'institutionalising' the knowledge base by sucking it out of heads and putting it onto servers and Intranets. Most large firms have now made significant investments in this area. On the other hand, there has been a lot of energy expended in trying to quantify the value of knowledge so that it can be capitalised on the balance sheet. As any good knowledge-consultant will tell you, the average ratio of goodwill to net asset value has never been higher.

These efforts on the whole have not delivered on the promise. Knowledge remains resolutely human in nature. Networks are facilitators not substitutes. Knowledge as an abstract asset is not the real source of competitive advantage for most firms. Banks of data, even if they sit on a server rather than on a library shelf, do not make a firm smart.

The source of competitive advantage for most successful firms is, in fact, knowledgeable people. It all comes down to flesh and blood. As one CEO eloquently put it at a conference on the subject, 'It's motivated brains, not supercharged silicon that make the difference.'[3] Knowledge in people's heads can be put to use; it is alive. Knowledge on disk is data. Data is by definition dead – an artefact.

So if it's all about people, what's the score out there in the market? If you ask your average employee about their level of commitment to their firm the response will be salutary. With the first waves of restructuring in the late 1980s, morale was at an all-time low. However, having now experienced either first hand or indirectly the results of reengineering, merger or outsourcing, most employees have broken the negativism barrier. It is no longer personal despair and pulling out of hair. We have now moved on. Now most employees have become pragmatic. If employers can't be relied upon, you have to rely on yourself. The savvy knowledge-worker is concerned about their own career, development of their skills and their personal equity, independent of their immediate employer. It is every man and woman for himself – in the most constructive manner of course!

The fundamental expression of this new pragmatism is job mobility. In 1980 the average white-collar worker had remained with their firm for twelve years. The average knowledge worker now only stays put for five years. As one employee of a reengineering weary commercial bank put it to me, 'You've got to invest in yourself. That's what counts. And don't kid yourself anyone else it going to do it for you.'[4] If you as a senior manager doubt it, take a poll. You will be shocked.

So what? Does it matter that the average employee has a pragmatic relationship with their firm? That they cannot articulate its hallowed list of 'values', let alone believe in them? Differentiation depends on people, their creativity and emotional commitment, not reengineered processes, not how good the M&A team is or how efficiently the consultants can cut out costs. So the answer is yes! Absolutely it matters!

---

[3] Panelist at Financial Times Conference on Knowledge Management in London, 1998.

[4] Senior relationship manager at a major US retail bank in Boston.

Most firms face a fundamental challenge when it comes to organic growth. Not surprising. After two mergers, a downsizing project and an intensive outsourcing programme, what is left of the company? What does it stand for? What is its culture? What is there for employees to believe in, to drive for? After ten years of reengineering, what relationship do employees have with the company? What role does the company have in their lives? If it is nothing but a loose collection of people with temporary allegiance behind a brand, what does this imply for growth? If it is better to be a consultant than an employee, what does this imply for commitment of energy? As one annual audit of employee attitudes put it, 'It is disturbing to report such an erosion of loyalty amongst internal customers when most firms are so avowedly pursuing loyalty campaigns with their external customers.' In ten years of non-organic change, most companies are beginning to hit the wall of how to drive the business forward. The average employee, the bedrock of creativity and energy, is very much less than fully committed.

The seven waves of change have played their role over the past decade and an important role, but efficiency measures as a source of competitive advantage are basically exhausted. The last wave has broken without materially moving the ship forward. Sure, the average manager has been 'empowered'. She has to manage a divisional P&L on a monthly basis against a budget she helps create. Some 20 per cent of her pay is variable, dependent on hitting budget. Half of this pays out in stock, linking her fate to that of the company. The mechanistic process of decentralised performance frameworks has been instituted. But does the evidence strongly suggest she feels driven to pour her soul into the firm? That the emotional commitment is there? The answer? No!

Emotional commitment directly drives the long-term ability of a firm to differentiate itself and secure competitive advantage. It is no good a firm producing one breakthrough product a decade. It has to evolve breakthrough concepts every couple of years. The rate of competitive innovation has never been greater. Nor has the finitude of the average life-cycle of a product. The battle to differentiate has never been harder. The only thing that will enable one firm to succeed over another with some certainty over a ten-year period will be the quality, dedication and drive of its people.

There can be no question of the vast potential to create value out of virtually every self-respecting and moral individual in a corporation today. The question is, how to tap this collective potential? Most firms have now placed 'HR issues' high on the agenda. To that end they have instituted aggressive share option programmes, espoused a philosophy of broad share ownership, invested in internal communications programmes, and made career management a priority. But most of these undertakings are 'programmes'. Programmes by definition are discrete undertakings. They tend to be tactical, short-term, with ever-changing flavours reflecting evolving management tastes. That does not constitute a unifying philosophy (or indeed strategy) that binds and defines an organisation.

Of course, intellectually 'putting the boot in' to these well-intentioned approaches is all very well, but it does not take us forward. How, then, should firms shake off this malaise, how should they regain momentum? Is it a new corporate strategy? Is it some newfangled creativity fad? This book argues that the way forward is intellectually a simple one. It centres on the emotional relationship between employee and firm and electrifying or recharging that relationship. It is not about strategy, it is not about M&A, it is not about knowledge management. It is about collective human drive. This we call reinspiration – a cohesive philosophy that defines how to electrify the relationships that bind a firm together.

We posit that reinspiration is the next great structural shift that will succeed the seven waves of change. The reinspired corporation is a corporation that has mastered how to command the full emotional and spiritual drive of its people and is positioned to reap the incomparable benefits. It appreciates that the strength of the bond between its people is the DNA. If the DNA is right, the other good things will surely follow. The reinspired corporation recognises the opportunity to plug the gap of meaning in our lives – to give us collective purpose and reward. Whether the firm expands into electronics or

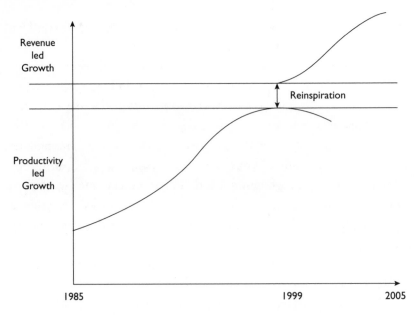

Revenue
led
Growth

Reinspiration

Productivity
led
Growth

1985   1999   2005

The next wave: the role of reinspiration

pulp, it will be a vibrant organisation. In an age where the only significant capital is the brain power of employees, the reinspired corporation will win. This book provides the tools that will help the beleaguered, strategy-weary firm get there – to reinspire itself.

1

The reinspiration model

What is a reinspired corporation?

If you've ever approached Chartres Cathedral by car across the corn-fields of the Loire, then you will know what an inspired building is like. The lofty apse rises almost 200 feet above the gilded, undulating surface of the fields, the flying buttresses silhouetted in their impossible act of levitation against the blue sky. The interior is like a vast cavern where the world's revolutions have finally been stilled by an act of colossal will. Whatever you may feel about old buildings no-one can refute that this one is inspired.

It was finished in 1224. It had taken 30 years to complete after a catastrophic fire in 1194 – roughly the same as the average life of a modern corporation. And what was extraordinary was how, over such an extended period of time, it was actually assembled. The work-force were largely volunteers, drawn from the local communities for 400 miles around. They worked virtually for free, devotedly – hauling stone for the masons to shape, straining over pulleys, preparing mortar. Some 3 000 000 stones in total, weighing over 500 000 tons, all moved and hewn by hand! This mass of material they crafted into a monument of unrivalled weightlessness; of serene, undisturbed space. When the Black Prince, son of Edward III, first saw it almost a 150 years after it was completed he called it 'a work of God'.

So what drove these several thousand barely paid souls to toil for so long to construct something that they could neither own nor which would ever bear any of their names? Were they simply crazy? The answer of course is that they were driven by a shared vision – the fulfilment of something in which they all consummately believed. Something beyond the daily grind of their lives; something that validated the unrewarded toil; something they believed in fully. They called it Faith.

The fact they were Christians was incidental in relation to the issues that concern us. What that achievement, like so many others, confirms is what is possible if people believe strongly enough in what they are doing. If the human soul buys into an idea with a passion, with total commitment, the bounds of what we are collectively capable are quite simply astounding. We all have that potential in us to build a Chartres. None of us can do it alone. But if incentivised appropriately we can together. History is littered with examples.

Now back to the company. What would it be like for a company of 50 000 souls if they were as single-mindedly driven to do what they did at Chartres? What would AT&T look like? IBM? ABB? Does any counterpart exist in the corporate world? Perhaps Microsoft, perhaps Sony? An equivalent is hard to find. This book argues that it is quite possible for the corporation to inspire and harness comparable committed, co-ordinated energy. This process we call 'reinspiration'.

A reinspired corporation is one where the majority of people working in the firm are committed to it with a passion. They understand its mission, they have bought into its ethos. For them the most important thing is that this belief should be vindicated. That the firm should soar. And as it soars, that they should feel a level of fulfilment that only absolute identification with the purpose brings. They are prepared to make enormous sacrifices for this goal. Indeed, the goal conditions the way they choose to live. Their motive is not simply money – money is merely a by-product that flows naturally as a result of far more gratifying achievements. The collective commitment of this group of people, sustained over time, results in an outpouring of creativity combined with productivity that makes the competitive position of the firm almost unassailable.

Does this sound like many firms you can name? Not many? Perhaps some of the newer, high-growth businesses fuelled by innovation and the charisma of a founder – Virgin, SAP, Yahoo, Starbucks, for example? Most firms appear to have forgotten that the only thing that drives earnings growth is their ability to harness the passions of their people. Period. The contract linking the individual to the company has been broken. The modern corporation is better described as a 'talent node' – a point of energy which by virtue of size, reputation and wealth pulls talented people into its sphere. As soon as these people collectively lose interest or the fate of the company wanes, the node dissipates and the essentially mobile resources move off. The mutual commitment of the firm to its people and vice versa has been so badly tattered it is on the verge of evaporating. The firm lacks 'inspiration'.

'Corporate faith'

The reinspired corporation is one where key people all share a common drive to a shared goal that might be called, for lack of a better word, 'faith'. The quasi-religious intimations of the term 'faith' may sound strange in the corporate context. Religion has almost become a taboo – a socially embarrassing anachronism. It makes us squirm, feel awkward. The sort of faith we are talking about – the emotional commitment to a supernal goal – does indeed borrow much from the classical religions. As we will explore presently, firms have much to learn from the great religions. They are, after all, the single most successful institutions binding together human beings behind common interests the planet has ever known. When measured in terms of market share, they are well ahead of the nation-state!

Corporate reinspiration is the binding together of individual and collective interests behind the goals of corporate advancement. It is the final and most powerful competitive dimension. A reinspired corporation will exude 'faith' – a conviction that is palpable. 'If they buy into its dreams, they will pour their hearts into making it better . . .' as Howard Schultz, Starbuck's CEO, put it.

'Corporate community'

Faith is the output, the after-glow. It is not the foundation, nor is it the fabric. The fabric of a strong firm is its 'community'. Corporate reinspiration is founded on the notion of 'community'. A community is a grouping of people and institutions which share common ideas and feelings on important issues. A community is bound together by a shared identity and 'values' (we will talk about the weakness of this term presently).

Communities tend to have fuzzy edges; they are not as clearly defined as a club or a tribe. People drift in and out; sometimes leaving for a while, only to return much later in their lives. Communities also tend to tolerate fairly diverse groups of people, sometimes comprised of sub-groups which may vary from each other quite dramatically.

Modern communities tend to be more dispersed culturally and geographically then they ever were historically. Perhaps the most extreme contemporary expression of the concept of community are the popular special interest sites on the Internet. Geocities calls itself a community – a community of people spread across the globe, the vast majority of whom will never interact with their fellow members other than through a wire and screen.

The concept of community is a powerful but troubled one in the corporate context. Corporate communities, like social communities, have changed dramatically. The inexorable process of globalisation among most larger firms has meant that they can no longer rely on social commonality conditioned by where they happen to be headquartered. The IBM company occupying an entire mid-Western town no longer dictates the basis of social cohesion in the firm. The modern firm faces the challenge of trying to corral peoples dispersed across dozens of countries into some coherent 'culture' (again, we will discuss the limitations of this term presently). Around 55 per cent of the Fortune 500's manufacturing is now done by overseas subsidiaries. The strain on the traditional definition of community has never been greater.

If the definitions of community are being stretched within companies, they are being stretched even further between companies. From the 1920s onwards most large firms ensured control over upstream and downstream industries through vertical integration. The recent disassembly of the vertically integrated combines has been dramatic, culminating in the core competencies crusade. In the place of ties of ownership, with concomitant threads of common culture, most businesses now depend on developing good relationships with their independent upstream and downstream partners – their enlarged community.

The same is true of the consolidated conglomerates. Conglomeratisation really hit its stride in the 1950s with the birth of the portfolio. Often the businesses bundled into portfolios shared common processes, R&D or used integrated distribution channels. While the past decade has all been about the disassembly of these groups, the old ties of idea exchange, distribution sharing and joint ventures still endure in many cases. The explosion of outsourcing on the tail of the core competencies whirlwind has rendered the quality of the links between discrete businesses all the more important. Increasingly the boundaries between individual businesses are blurring. The relationship between a major corporation and its network of independent suppliers, distributors and even competitors is no longer clear-cut. The community of the corporation extends outside the perimeter of its own payroll. The question is, how to define what this enlarged community stands for and how to make it cohere? For it is the degree of coherence of the community of the firm that will drive its long term success.

'Corporate ethos'

So what binds a community together? What is the fundamental glue? Most analysts if posed this question will resort to a description of a firm's 'values'. 'Values' is a comfortable term because values can be enumerated in the form of a list; we believe in great customer service, honesty, helping the community, equal rights, quality in everything we do, etc.

The obvious point about such lists is that they all tend to be the same. Johnson and Johnson's credo has clearly been important to the culture of the firm. But it does not differ in vast degree from that of Motorola, IBM, 3M or a dozen other Fortune 500 firms. In reality, none of us are united as a community by something as specific as a list of values. We are bound together by something far more inchoate and subtle. That is not to say that the list of values is not relevant. They certainly are. But they are only part of the magic glue and wildly simplistic as an attempt to encapsulate the stuff that makes up a community.

The other common favourite of the consultants is the concept of culture. It is certainly the case that strong communities tend to have common habits that might be encapsulated in the term culture. But the reality is that most sizeable communities encompass a myriad of cultures, whether as a result of the ethnic origins of their members or the other personal communities of family or belief their members also belong to. We all belong to more than one community, although perhaps only one work community. Strong communities absorb these differences, just as Islam retains its relevance from Indonesia to Asia Minor, and even to Bradford. Whatever the cultural influences of strong communities, they share standards and ambitions that transcend these differences. They fulfil supernal goals and provide transcendent meaning in the lives of all individual members.

A more useful term than either values or culture is 'ethos'.[1]

---

[1] Drawn from the Greek, it literally means the 'character' of a community and particularly a religious one.

A coherent community shares a common ethos, a way of seeing things, a character that conditions behaviour and defines acceptable and unacceptable social norms. Ethos is broad, deep and almost impossible to define. It is manifested in people's behaviour, their language and the way they conduct their daily business lives. Whatever their culture and background, the community of the firm instils and demands shared standards – a common ethos – on the important issues.

A community, defined by a common ethos, is a coherent, powerful force. In a supercharged community, one with great coherence, this ethos will have an added glow to it, a glow which makes it inspirational rather than simply a moderating force. This glow we have termed faith. Faith is a spark that turns a loosely knit community into an animated, driven force.

Corporate reinspiration is about turning the individual constituents of a company into a driven, 'evangelistic' community. Corporate reinspiration is not really a strategy at all in a conventional sense. It is not focused on either a structural or process view of the business. It is not about shifting the organisation of departments, it is not about reshuffling the flow of work. Nor is it about shifting portfolios of assets. What it says is that an organisation will do best over the medium and long term if it focuses on harnessing the collective drive of its employees within the framework of a broad strategic direction. It says that the key driver of the rate of innovation and differentiation will be the level of motivation of its people to achieve a shared vision, to fulfil a common sense of purpose. It says that an organisation that is differentiated will be founded on a strong community, with a shared ethos and imbued with a drive we have called, for lack of a better word, faith.

That is all very well. Nobody (we assume) is going to argue with the objective. The explosion of management literature on the subject of motivation and knowledge management is testimony to the preoccupation of executives with such ideas. The big issue is how to do something about it. How can a large collection of dispersed people be transformed into a driven community inspired by common purpose?

Figure 1.1 The foundations of a reinspired firm

Reinspiration benchmarking

So where do we turn to learn how to do it? Surely some firm out there is reinspired? The benchmarking quest begun by *In Search of Excellence*,[2] and more recently taken up in *Built to Last*,[3] has become something of a search for the Holy Grail. Each time a corporation is held up as a paragon it has an uncanny habit of stumbling. The same firms continually re-emerge – Motorola, Boeing, 3M, Merck, P&G, etc. – all of them among the Fortune 100. By definition, they are firms that have in broad terms 'made it'. The search for competitive advantage can easily deteriorate into a process of emulation of whoever is the top dog at the time.

But clearly this is not correct. The firms that were the top dogs 20 years ago are not the same as today. Most have been displaced, changed name via merger or otherwise morphed and disappeared. The average life of the Fortune 500 firm is short. The average life of the large firm as top dog is even shorter.

This being the case, what confidence can we have that today's hot companies reliably exemplify what will constitute success going forward? This is glaringly apparent when we think of what businesses are commonly (and in many cases rightly so) exalted by consultants

---

[2] See Peters, Tom and Waterman, Robert. *In Search of Excellence.* Warner Books, 1988.

[3] See Porass, Jerry J. and Collins, James C. *Built to Last.* Harper Business, 1994.

and in the management literature. IBM, Motorola and 3M, for example, are all essentially product manufacturing businesses. They deal in hard assets, return on capital employed and distribution. The truly high growth businesses tend to have few tangible assets at all. Andersen Consulting has grown at a compound rate of 30 per cent for the last decade and now turns over around $8 billion. Microsoft, the world's most valuable company, is essentially nothing but a collection of talented people. Goldman Sachs, the business that has perhaps created the greatest wealth for its top hundred employees in history through its recent IPO, watches its assets walk out of the elevator each night. In a Western economy driven increasingly by knowledge assets, the new competitors are probably only just emerging. GE may itself ultimately become a pure professional services firm. So, for that matter, might IBM!

If the corporate world cannot offer reliable paragons of reinspiration, which world can? Which world has given rise to institutions, to communities, that are truly global, which bind large, culturally diverse groups together behind a shared ethos, which have endured longer than a hundred years and which truly inspire dedication? There is only one answer. The institutions that have shown themselves best at cultivating community, driving through collective ethos, crowning it with the devoted emotional commitment called faith, and hence succeeding as tremendous institutional forces, are not businesses at all. Businesses, on the whole, have not shown themselves as masters of this process. The only communities that can lay claim to that achievement are, in fact, the great religious movements.

It is our contention that perhaps the best examples of how to achieve reinspiration are the world's religions. If they are examined in detail, the world's seven great religions share a number of common characteristics in terms of how they unify and inspire their vast communities. These can be condensed into a model of reinspiration. It is this model and its application to the corporation that we will examine in detail in this book.

This is certainly not to say that a corporation should become religious; that executives should become 'tree huggers'. The increasingly common term 'corporate religion' is almost absurd! Businesses do not serve the functions of religions, not should they. The point simply is that there are excellent lessons to be learned from the most successful institutions on earth about getting people engaged in the long term.

Taking a leaf out of the book of the great religions

The world's seven great religions – namely, Christianity, Judaism, Hinduism, Confucianism, Taoism, Buddhism and Islam – between them account for a following of over 75 per cent of the world's population in one or other of their many manifestations. They have all endured in a form not far removed in essence from their original manifestation for an average of over 1500 years, although in their societal role they have evolved, sometimes quite dramatically. That survival rate compares to an average Fortune 100 life span of 42 years. It also compares to the average age of the sovereign state of around 200 years.

While elsewhere in the world religion is still the defining societal force, in the West, and particularly Northern Europe, religion is somewhat dismissed as a spent force. Few English or German people under the age of 40 ever go to church. Churchgoers are stereotyped as over 50, blue-rinse, suburbanites, attributable with the glamour of tax accountants! However, even in the agnostic West this stereotype is misleading. The dominant national religion, whether Protestantism, Lutheranism or Catholicism, still defines the moral frameworks that unite these societies and drives their laws. Also we should not ignore the fact that in the US a stunning 30 per cent of the middle-class, white-collar population regularly attend religious service. That's more than watch CNN! At one evangelical extreme, Pat Robertson has a regular TV audience of around 16 million people!

The reason for their long-term success is that, as institutions, they satisfy a set of universal psychological needs. All of the great religions evolved over at least 1000-year period in response to fundamental needs, adapting to the changing environment until they hit on a 'formula' (in somewhat vulgar parlance) that worked. They have therefore had plenty of time to empirically discover what their 'customers' need. Once all the distractions are stripped away, they are the only organisations that can justly claim to have fastened upon the kernels of universal want.

Most corporations, by contrast, have achieved a collective history of no more than 50 years. Their level of collective understanding about their core constituents, their people, is infinitely less mature than that of the great religions. They engage in formal market research to accelerate the process, but virtually none of this is aimed at understanding themselves. It is aimed at understanding their external customers. The only systematic self-diagnosis most firms engage in is done by management consultants. This on the whole leads us back to the mechanistic approaches we enumerated in the introduction – you can't reengineer your soul!

So what is it that the great religions have mastered that has enabled them to corral such large masses into a position where they share a common ethos; a common ethos that drives such identification with group interests that, at one extreme, it has inspired martyrdom? What has enabled them to endure as definers of vast communities despite ever changing fashions and politics?

Seven common qualities

While immensely diverse in their practice and in the philosophical foundation of their observances, if all their particular qualities are stripped back, the great religious movements share seven common qualities through which they appear to inspire adherence in people:

1   They provide a context of moral authority and a framework which offers the chance for personal redemption.
2   They emphasise looking beyond the individual and the primacy of integration or surrender to collective interests for a good which is beyond limited self-interest.

3   They are characterised by deeply ingrained ritual and symbolism.
4   Their progress is founded on well-understood tradition.
5   They are essentially optimistic in their outlook; their view of the competitive universe is positive.
6   They encourage the asking of the big questions.
7   They cloak themselves in mystery; they are not easily understood.

These seven characteristics are so pervasive in all seven great movements and so fundamental to their character that there is every reason to believe they are there to satisfy a profound psychological need in all of us – whatever the name of the God or type of moral code we subscribe to. It is these set of needs which the great religions have learnt to satisfy more effectively than any other type of social institution on the planet, including the Nation State.

First universal need

The first universal need we all share is to perceive an order that puts definition on our individual efforts, which shows that we can contribute something that has meaning, that confirms that what we are doing is good, that there will be a reward for the trials and tribulations it involves. This is the salve to the incipient threat of futility we all face at one time or another every day of our lives. The context of moral authority is the necessary framework which provides some guarantee that the positive efforts we have put in will lead somewhere. That they will bring endorsement, recognition. That we should not simply stay in bed or ransack the shopping mall. That behaving properly is a better approach. That we should continue to strive.

In the case of the great religions, this authority is not only worldly, it is divine. It infuses our consciousness with a line of delineation – between the things we should feel good about and the things we should feel ashamed of. This context of moral authority tends to be so ingrained in one form or another in most of us that we don't perceive it as an ethos at all. We perceive it as a personal quality. That is testimony to its success in fashioning our motivations.

Second universal need

The second universal need we all have is to escape from the locked cell of our ego. We are all inclined to view the world from our own perspective of personal preoccupation. If an event occurs, from a collapse in the stock market to a hurricane in the West Indies, we will all tend to absorb the event from the perspective of it disrupting our retirement or our holiday plans. We might feel some remorse for the people victimised, but usually with reference to quiet personal relief we are not involved. How many of us will willingly lay down our own careers for the interest of the company?

Self-interest is, as we all now know, a natural corollary of biological selection. Darwin spotted that one – the selfish gene. But it is also profoundly limiting and unsettling. Unique self-focus means that individual setbacks assume vast proportions. That we can derive no real joy from collective success. That our relationship with others is always tainted with competitiveness: 'Sure, I'm glad for him, but just perhaps I'd like to see him fall flat on his face.'

The product of competitiveness is isolation – him versus me. The next 20 years promise to be characterised by extreme individual competitiveness. The emphasis on socialised competitiveness has never been greater. They also promise to be the most lonely and divorced years for many of us. Separation appears not to be a natural condition. We are all social creatures at heart. As well as admiration, we all crave companionship. That is why extreme competition produces psychological dysfunctionality.

The question is, what possible point of connection can we forge in our competitive world where we are ranked one against another? Are we doomed to competitive isolation? The great religions say no. Community, shared beliefs, alignment with collective interest are the dominant psychological needs; more dominant than the drive for individual accomplishment. This would suggest we have our role models all wrong. The obsessive focus on individualism, on competitiveness is actually a mistake. We all long for a higher collective purpose; a reunification. This in fact leads to greater success. A little like focusing on measuring profit rather than what produces it, focusing on competition puts the cart before the horse.

Third universal need

The third common need we all share is for the security of ritual. Our lives are fundamentally ritualised; through from the daily routine of waking and preparing for work, to the habit of slumping at night in a favourite chair. The act of repetition reassures us that life is predictable, controllable; that what we do has an order that is both enduring, meaningful and which is something worth fighting to perpetuate.

The most powerful rituals are, however, social rituals – where we act out something that expresses a common thread shared between us and where participating in the act reinforces a sense of belonging, a relief from isolation. Social ritual permeates our lives, through from football matches to debutante balls.

Ritual is religion's cradle. Religion rose out of celebration and its nemesis bereavement, both of which call out for public expression. When something good happens or when we are smitten we want to share it with others to give it meaning. Ritualised acts channel this desire and by externalising it make it real. The great religions have mastered the power of ritual. They are among the most ritualised institutions to have ever appeared. Whether you are a Western churchgoer or not, the rituals espoused by the great religions will permeate your life – through from the great annual celebrations of Easter and Christmas to the way we handle death.

Closely bound up with ritual is the process of enactment. All religious rituals act out the seminal events that gave rise to them.

None of us are as motivated by an abstract idea as we are by something tangible, something enacted. We are drawn to Soaps about life's surreality like *Ally McBeal* more than we are to reading Jean Paul Sartre. The process of enactment, of extemporisation, draws us in. For a moral order to be sustained it has to take on a form which compels us, which we can feel and which we can see acted out. The process of re-enactment reinforces meaning. That is why religion is full of ritualised enactments, of ceremony.

The by-product of such ritual is symbolism. Symbolism makes complex ideas concrete and thereby real. If they are concrete we can also control ideas that might otherwise overwhelm us. Whether we live in Kathmandu or Kentucky we all know broadly speaking what is signified by a crucifix or a five-pointed star, even if we are not versed in the doctrine underlying it. It connotes a meaning and describes a community of which we might or might not wish to be a part. The great religions have all turned the convoluted, abstract language of religious philosophy into a universalistic language of symbols, accessible and compelling even to the illiterates that comprise 40 per cent of the world's population. Their language is universally intelligible.

Fourth universal need

The fourth common need is to know where we come from. The Mormons' website on genealogy scores as many hits as any single part of Yahoo. Historical continuity is a profound psychological need. We also need to believe we come from a good past that endorses our present. We all like to think well of our forebears. It is part of a healthy self-image. As a result we tend to give great credence to the past. This may sound anachronistic in an age where change is meteoric and the past tends to be dismissed as arcane. But psychologically, continuity is a foundation stone of our sense of order. Our traditions make us secure. That as why, when push comes to shove, communities will defend them even to the death.

The evidence that something has worked in the past is also a powerful motivator. It brings the endorsement that this order has served generations before us – that it is not some dull contrivance. Tradition preserves what past generations have learnt and bequeaths it to the present as a blueprint for how to get by. It shows that what we are doing bears the proof of having served people before us who were better than us. It therefore gives us something to live up to, and to pass on.

The great religions have mastered the management of heritage better than any other institution. They define the history that gave rise to them. They enshrine a tradition that reassures us that we have a viable past, and that this is worth fighting for in order that we might bequeath it to our children. To prevent it wilting, they keep it alive through story-telling and fable. It is such a powerful motivator that, given the wrong circumstances, it has driven whole peoples to war to defend those traditions.

Fifth universal need

The fifth common need we all share is to feel that there is something better we can strive for, that positive efforts will be positively rewarded. The absence of the possibility of self-improvement, whether morally or materially, ultimately saps any sense of drive, of optimism. People who are resigned to the status quo, for whatever reason, tend to be negative. They lack life-force. Whether through forced retirement, social exclusion, classism or racism, the lack of the possibility of self-advancement is fundamentally debilitating. That is why for the several hundred years there was feudalism in Europe, up until the Renaissance, nothing happened – it was literally a Dark Age. It is the resulting despair of exclusion among certain ethnic minorities that produces the social violence so familiar in many US cities.

The great religions ultimately take the view that good is on our side; that the future is worth fighting for however bad the present. They completely reject passivity, fatalism, and resignation – the three most corrosive forces that stunt productivity. The great religions militate for advancement, for hope. As we will explore, Judaism in particular, which is perhaps the most influential religion on Western thought, sides firmly with the underdog and proposes a philosophy of self-betterment. It propounds that there is something worth getting out of bed to battle for each day.

Sixth universal need

The sixth trait we all share is the need to ask; satisfying our curiosity is one of the most fundamental traits of human beings. Apparently, even our distant ancestors – the chimpanzees – are more motivated to find out what is on the other side of a closed door than they are by the prospect of food or even sex! The process of questioning is closely bound up with a sense of progress, of optimism that there are things waiting to be found and which through patient study can ultimately be understood. The process of enquiry is, broadly speaking, synonymous with the process of human advancement.

The great religions propound that there are important questions about purpose and meaning which we should not be afraid to ask. Religion tries to both arouse and point us in the direction of resolving the imponderable questions of where we come from, of what is our role on this earth. The process of asking is cathartic and invites the belief that, although imperfectly understood, there is a reason to the world if only we had the patience and clarity of mind to understand it. We continue asking and seeking because we trust that answers will ultimately be found and the path is a rewarding one.

Religion fundamentally encourages, not discourages the process of questioning. It begs us not to be afraid to ask (contrary to common misgivings about rigid doctrine which all too often reflects the interests of those interpreting religion and politicising it, rather than being a reflection of religion itself). For a thousand years religious learning was the keystone of intellectual advancement. It is only relatively recently that the state educational system has assumed this mantel.

Such questioning now actually threatens to discredit religious doctrine – how can anyone really turn water to wine and how can I therefore believe a word of it? But doctrine is not the same as the religion of which it is an interpretation at one point in time. Darwin has not answered the big question of the meaning of life. We continue to ask.

Seventh universal need

The seventh common quality is that we all appear to have a profound need for mystery, to believe that there are forces that we can only dimly understand. That there is more out there than we can possibly grasp. If the world was completely intelligible, if there wasn't the promise of things we have not yet seen, then it would indeed be a dull place. There would be no room for advancement, no room for revelation, no room for redemption. The existence of mystery is closely bound up with optimism and positivism. In the absence of satisfactory mystery, we invent it, from ET to ESP. Recognising the limits of our abilities to perceive, to comprehend, is essential to assure us that there is no limit to how far we can go – should we be smart enough.

The great religions cloak themselves in mystery. Their origins are opaque; their progenitors miracle workers; their vision less than accessible. Their pervasive use of symbolism and ritual in place of terse statement of fact reinforces the ambiguity. In a world which is brutally simple in terms of material power, this ambiguity leaves a space for redemption, where there is the possibility of something wonderful happening. That's what keeps us going!

So, what's the real score out there?

The great religions all respond directly to these seven seminal psychological needs. Indeed, it would appear that they are structured around that objective – leading people down their seven paths. This targeted responsiveness has given them tremendous power as collective bodies. It has made them the ultimate point of definition; the structure proscribing what their subscribers believe in. Even for the most adamantly atheist of us, at times of need when the logical answers fail us, we all turn to some concept of faith.

Most institutions (as opposed to real communities!), whether religious houses or corporations, fail to deliver on one or all of these counts. It is their failure to respond to these seminal needs that appears to undermine their success as organisations. All such social structures appear to crumble on a mixture of the same grounds:

Seminal needs

First seminal failure

Authority tends to become personalised, vested in the hierarchy, 'hereditary', or defined by individuals anxious to retain power. Authority which is personalised and not institutionalised as a moral framework serves short-term ambitions. It is neither likely to meet the needs of the individuals in that community nor has much chance of lasting. An individual might carry a large group of people with them for a while by force of personality. However, the set of values they represent will not become an ethos; they will crumble. Doesn't this sound a familiar situation? It is for this reason that most corporations succumb within a single human lifetime. It is all about the CEO, not the community of the company.

Second seminal failure

The organisation fragments into splinter groups of intense self-interest. The framework holding them together is overpowered by the impetus towards individual autonomy, towards individual recognition. Groups of individuals break away to start their own endeavours. Through a process of attrition the old core withers.

In the case of the great religions, whilst this same process has happened, the splinter groups have tended to retain a strong blueprint of their original. Protestantism which has fractured into innumerable groups in the US, for example, still collectively appears to retain a uniform creed. The same is not true of companies. The parts typically become predators of their progenitor. Lucent turns on AT&T, Microsoft on IBM, Andersen Consulting on Arthur Andersen. The intense focus on individualism is totally compelling (and probably fuelled in part as a social phenomenon by the intense personality worship of the sports, film and media industries). Once unleashed it is almost irreversible. In today's business world it is endemic. But it is not the way to build a powerfully entity founded on a cohesive community.

Third seminal failure

Rituals become mechanical. The purpose behind them is lost and they no longer carry meaning. They are obeyed as an extension of a set of orders, unthinkingly. Any ritual that is meaningless will ultimately die, like an unused limb, and fall away into irrelevance. It will not act to hold a group of people together. It will also be subject to misappropriation by leaders or managers defending their own interests. Symbols will, in such an environment, be deployed tactically through identity programmes, to further the self-aggrandising plans of a senior management group anxious to stamp their mark. They become logos – almost like personal cartouches; 'So and so is in charge and don't forget it!'

Fourth seminal failure

Tradition is used to buttress the status quo against the threats posed by change. As such, it relentlessly loses relevance and drags the organisation down. The ability to bring in fresh blood dries up, the ability to grow the quality people deteriorates and, with the stifling dominance of the old guard, the prospect of change grows ever more remote. Tradition becomes static and ossified to the point of being unintelligible to the majority of participants. The only way the chains are broken is through eventual crisis, chronic angina, before open heart surgery is finally administered. These are the symptoms most habitually associated with corporate death.

Fifth seminal failure

Genuine enquiry deteriorates into bureaucratic hair splitting, so that the important questions are skirted and the status quo fundamentally unquestioned. Memos go out and endless debate is stimulated about trivial questions. There is an obsession with the details of propriety and form. The big, seminal issues go unanswered. No one is allowed to pose the big, troubling questions. The organisation becomes myopic, introverted and ultimately blind.

Sixth seminal failure

A positive sense of purpose, of mission is lost and replaced with rumours and speculation. The sense of forward motion is stalled. The focus is on averting the risk of any fundamental, unsettling change. It is defined by a set of possible negative outcomes. The top dogs are firmly out to save their own skins, whatever the costs. For the rest, the most positive outcome is no outcome. Change is seen as scary. People prefer to defend what they have than seize any opportunity. The organisation becomes sclerotic.

Seventh seminal failure

The fallibility's and failings of the organisation are transparent to all but those inside who refuse to wake up and smell the coffee. The aura it once had is faded. The characters on whom it was founded are exposed as less than wholesome. The best graduates hold no illusion about the firm. The analysts have crawled all over it, along with the investment bankers and consultants. It is rich pickings for advisors. There is no mystery at all – no allure.

Do any of these situations sound familiar? Most firms that perform indifferently, decline or are subject to take-over will tend to have some clear market deficiencies. Their products might be tarnished, their unit costs high, their share of voice poor, their financials flagging. But these are all symptoms, not causes. Most analysts and, indeed, most managers focus on symptoms – they are tangible, measurable and discrete. Causes are always much tougher to identify. They are systemic, intangible and complex. But at heart they usually come down to the same seven core deficiencies – the flip-side of the seven paths of reinspiration. It is the ability of the firm to achieve and instil a powerful, cohesive community of smart people that will determine its fate. That ability appears to rest on its mastery of the seven paths.

Like all things, organisations whether religious or demotic go through cycles of decay and renewal. The great religions, no less than corporations, have all gone through long cycles – a process of stultification which precipitates revolution and then back again. In the case of religion, the reaction of Buddha to the stultification of Hinduism, or the Protestantism of Martin Luther in the face of the rigid anachronism of German Catholicism were all twists in long term organic cycles. In each case the restoration of the community appears to turn on the re-establishment of the same seven fundamental characteristics. It is on these that institutional renewal appears to pivot.

Back to the corporation

It all sounds very good but what does this mean for the way corporations are managed? Translating the same seven qualities to the world of the corporation is in fact fairly straight forward. It posits that the successful firm is characterised by:

1   A framework of moral authority that binds the community of the firm together behind a unified purpose. Every party to it feels infused with a virtuous ambition to propagate the firm's way of doing things. The correct path is clear, even if it is not without its immense challenges.

2   An environment which obviates the need for continual self-questioning by employees and allows for close identification with group interests. No one is eaten by self-doubt or reservations about what they are doing. The task is clear and it is shared. Participation in it is exhilarating.

3   Absolute clarity of identity. There is no mistaking the firm in any of its manifestations. To the members of the community of the firm, its identity is a rich, cohesive language that connotes a like-minded way of thinking among its constituents – even if it sometimes results in aggressive debate. Participating in that language provides self-validation.

4   A keen sense by the community of the firm of where it has come from and what it stands for. Participation in shaping that heritage in the future lends all members a level of purpose – a reason to strive to propagate the community – which perhaps they were not born with in their personal lives.

5   An essentially optimistic view of the world. The firm provides a positive set of aspirations about the collective future for everyone involved. It confirms at every turn that the future is worth fighting for.

6   An intense level of enquiry and debate about objectives and goals that dispels the status quo and keeps the process of re-invention

moving ahead of the industry. It is not shy of constructive dissent. It fosters competitive internal trading of ideas.

7   An aura of unquantifiableness which means that it is perceived as more than a producer of a good or service. Its *raison d'être* is higher. The best people aspire to be part of the club.

These qualities are comparatively abstract and seminal. Certainly they are very different from the set of drivers of competitiveness on which most business analysts focus. As we hope to convince you, they are collectively the fundamental source of competitive advantage for any community, whether in the business of religion or selling car tyres. Mastering them leads to reinspiration.

Summary

We are not proposing that in order to succeed corporations should go religious (indeed, if anything, it is religions that are going increasingly into business). Nor are we suggesting that corporations need develop their own religions – unless the CEO is inclined towards monomania! There are a bundle of emotions and goals peculiar to the religious life which are quite distinct from the demands of life at work and the exigencies of the average company battling it out in the aluminium or margarine industries. Success in business cannot be achieved through genuflection.

What we do propose, however, is that the process of simply benchmarking against competitor firms or other industries will not provide break-through insights. Insights into efficiency and cost management – the most conducive to conventional benchmarking – are all but exhausted. All that will emerge is inevitable parity and sameness. Instead there are communities which have proved themselves extraordinarily successful over long periods of time at capturing the hearts and minds of their managers and followers. These communities, the seven great religions, have had an average of 1500 years apiece to distil the best ways of winning souls by responding to what

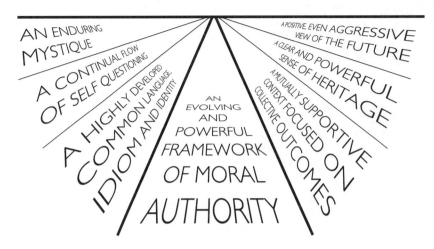

Figure 1.2 **The seven paths to reinspiration**

ultimately matters most to human beings. Distilling these learnings into one concept we have called reinspiration – literally the means to lift people up to better things.

So, if it isn't some waffly diatribe about values and culture, what is corporate reinspiration? It is a strategy, and like any formalistic strategy it comes with a set of tools, a framework. This framework recognises that intelligent human beings are driven to extraordinary collective endeavours by a confluence of forces – forces which are the fundamental determinants of social purpose. Any company ultimately is nothing more than a collection of individuals with a collective history. The reinspired organisation is one where the level of identification between the individual and the collective goals of the company is indivisibly close. This level of identification is the wellsource of successful differentiation.

Before we examine in detail the application of the reinspiration framework to the practical exigencies of the business world, there is one small hurdle to overcome – senior management mindsets! Any major change, including enlightenment, must start at the top.

2

The way corporations think about competitiveness: is there really a problem?

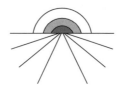

Shedding anachronistic mindsets

Any change in how a business is managed has inevitably to be preceded by a change in senior management mindsets. In the absence of social revolution, new ideas have to be espoused at the top. Perhaps the greatest obstacle to the adoption of corporate reinspiration are the frameworks we as senior managers all use to think about and analyse the competitiveness of our businesses – the frameworks that define our understanding of how firms compete. Unless these frameworks are dispensed with, a quantum leap forward in terms of performance is impossible. We are the prisoners of our own outdated frames of reference. Fundamentally these mental frameworks have not changed for 30 years. They have simply evolved at the margins. They are characterised by an emphasis on structure and process.

If most analysts or senior managers were asked to assess the cohesiveness and strength of a company they would probably first turn to outputs – its size in terms of revenues, growth in profits, EPS and market share. In other words, the standard indices commonly deployed to measure corporate might. (These have a well documented leaning to earnings in the West and market share in the East.) At a secondary level they would typically turn to measures of underlying productivity: sales per employee, cycle time, unit costs, time to market, etc. They might, if pressed harder, refer to the firm's history of innovation – how many cutting edge products it has brought to market, its position on the innovation curve. Ultimately, and only as a last recourse, they might somewhat uncomfortably allude to the woolly concepts of 'culture' and 'values'. But this is typically unsettling territory for analysts. It is too effeminate, too soft. It cannot be measured based on the audited accounts and industry reports.

If forced into this terrain, most analysts will retreat to the safer territory of a discussion about the strength of senior management and, in particular, the CEO. As we will explore, today's financial community is obsessed with ideas of individualism; the conviction that the performance of the company is largely driven by the individual at the top. The possibility that competitiveness is a far more complex human phenomenon is not a comfortable one.

All these indices are nothing but outputs. They are symptoms. They do not describe what drives performance. It is true, of course, that the management consulting industry has drilled down further. There have been a proliferation of models which attempt to describe what drives underlying performance. Probably the most pervasive model for describing the workings of the company, and the one which has spawned an army of derivatives, is the Value Chain.[1]

The Value Chain is essentially a structural description of the make-up of a company, breaking down its processes into value driving parts and applying a set of mensural indices to them. It is concerned with mechanics. It treats the firm as a machine – something that can be dissected like a specimen. The Value Chain is, in effect, the progenitor of the reengineering movement. When the pieces are understood they can be reshuffled, reengineered. On a more positive note, it is also, of course, a vital educational diagnostic as we explored

[1] See Porter, Michael E. *Competitive Advantage: Creating and Sustaining Superior Performance.* The Free Press, 1985.
[2] See Scott, Mark C. *Value Drivers: The Manager's Guide to Driving Corporate Value Creation.* John Wiley & Sons, 1999.

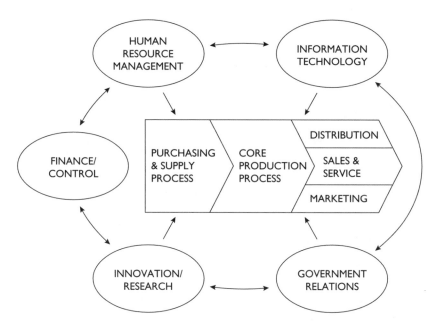

Figure 2.1 The generic value chain

in 'Value Drivers: The Manager's Guide to Driving Corporate Value Creation'.[2]

If the Value Chain is the structural description of the guts of a company, the most pervasive model for describing the competitive dynamics of the industry in which the firm competes is Michael Porter's 'Five Forces'.[3] Again, it simplifies an inherently complex world of human interactions into five measurable drivers. Such market models are useful frames of reference for understanding the way businesses compete and, again, we explored variants on such models as valuable and essential learning devices in *Value Drivers*. But as a means to direct companies for long-term competitiveness their efficacy is more limited. They turn relationships into structure, ignoring the human component. But make no mistake about it, all transactions are driven principally by relationships, not pure economics. The 'demand curve' assumes the world is without emotions. That is patently absurd!

---

[3] See Porter, Michael E. *Competitive Strategy: Techniques for Analysing Initiatives and Competitors.* The Free Press, 1980.

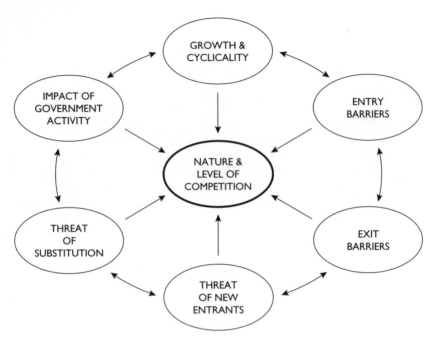

Figure 2.2 The generic market model

More recently the Balanced Scorecard has emerged as a method of leavening the focus on financial measures with gauges of process efficiency and client satisfaction.[4] Again, it is useful as a learning tool for managers. But it will not produce a dynamic, inspired company *per se*. Measurement can foster learning but to want to learn together people need to share an aspiration. We should not mistake tools for goals or for drivers.

The use of structures and processes to drive an understanding of a firm's competitiveness is akin to surgery in medicine. Surgery can take one a fair distance with regard to specific ailments; traumas can be eased, malfunctions patched up, clogged arteries by-passed. But surgery alone cannot provide a satisfactory explanation of why an

---

[4] See Kaplan, Robert S. and Norton, David P. 'Putting the Balanced Scorecard to Work'. *Harvard Business Review*, September/October 1993.

organism fails or succeeds. That bundle of drivers is far too complex for a structural, surgical view. It may be that the wounds are psychological. But even this explanation is generally a crude simplification of an intensely complex phenomenon called the human condition which is driven primarily by social relationships.

Along with the structural, mechanistic diagnosis of the corporation, there has evolved the parallel stream of analysis focused on individual psychology – the soft end of the spectrum. Borrowing from the world of clinical psychology, organisational behaviourialists tend to focus on individual motives. The big problem with psychology as a business tool is that it tends to devolve to the level of the individual. It is not a lever which senior management can pull to affect total organisational change. As any manager knows, individual motivations are quixotic, ever shifting. It is very tempting to propose that a firm should develop an ability to deal with employees individually – to provide flexible career structures; to provide flexible reward and incentive schemes. But at the end of the day it usually proves impracticable. It has the same smack of idealism as one-to-one marketing. The reality is that individualising a firm's dealings with both its internal and external customers is not a practical possibility and, in addition, something is lost in the attempt – a unified voice. Faced with these dilemmas, the inability of HR to provide answers has meant it has firmly remained the third wheel of business management, subjugated to the finance, operating and marketing people.

The practical challenge is to see beyond outputs – market share, and revenue growth – as indices of corporate health. It is also to see beyond the mechanics, the working parts of the organisation – cycle time, WIP, scrap rates, etc. Without getting mired down in the impractical issues of individual motivation, the challenge is to identify the levers that can shift the entire employee base in the direction of long-term competitive differentiation. But first the frame of reference has to change. The old idols must be torn down.

The old intellectual idols

The two dominant paradigms that have driven business thinking for the past 25 years have been what we could term the 'aggregational' and 'reductionist' movements. These two counter-movements are the seminal forces underlying the various structural and process models dreamt up by consultants over the past 20 years. Neither has anything to say about emotional motivation, what we have called 'reinspiration'. We would contend that reinspiration is the third fundamental movement in the evolution of management thinking that will play out over the next couple of decades.

Up until the early 1990s the diversified conglomerates dominated the corporate landscape – Hanson Trust, ITT, Mitsubishi, etc. Their essential claim was that they could leverage their management expertise across industries with similar operating economics. Fundamental to their philosophy was the argument that portfolios of assets with

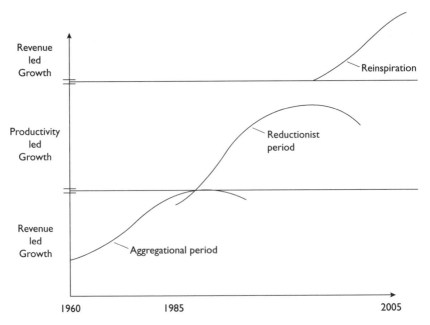

Figure 2.3 The underlying currents of change

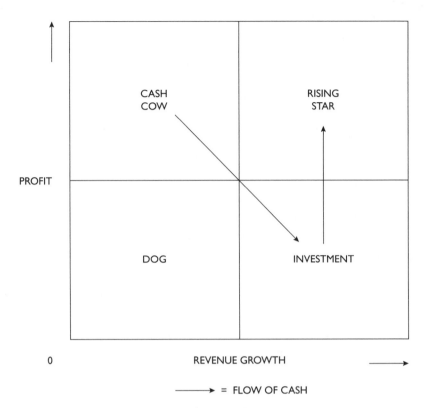

Figure 2.4 The BCG type portfolio matrix

different cash flow dynamics, and at different stages in their business development, could be run in a mutually reinforcing manner. In the now ubiquitous nomenclature of the Boston Consulting Group, the mature cash cows could fuel the growth of rising stars and so on. Their strategy was founded, consciously or unconsciously, on the example of vertical integration from the 1920s.

The aggregators also knew how to handle the markets better than individual businesses, centralising the core treasury function at the corporate level. As far as the capital markets were concerned, the higher level of sophistication of these holding structures in terms of balance sheet management, treasury, M&A and investor relations made them favoured beasts. Their cost of borrowing was typically lower and they had sufficient mass in the markets to finance continual streams of acquisitions, either via share placements or in shares.

While most of the major quoted aggregators, though not all (GE is one obvious example), have been broken up to differing extents on the anvil of core competencies, the aggregator strategy itself has not disappeared. The venture and private equity funds, and even banks such as Nomura, have taken up the mantel instead, although in a more discrete and private form, managing portfolios of companies in which they often have significant minority or even majority stakes scattered across wide ranges of sectors.

The point about diversified holdings, whether in the form of public companies or private funds, is that their typical focus is on extracting incremental value from existing assets, largely through balance sheet leverage. Their value added is not based on inspiring extraordinary motivation among employees to drive the business to future greatness. There is no intrinsic vision for people to buy into. The only logic is gleaning efficiencies that can be leveraged across businesses. The rationale is extrinsic.

The industrial aggregator strategy (as opposed to the financial portfolio strategy employed by the active funds) has now largely been discredited in Western markets after ruling the world-wide corporate scene in one guise or another since the 1960s. Even Korea and Japan have witnessed the slow process of unravelling of the *chaebol* and *kiretsu* with their bonds of mutual interest. The focus of most current management literature and management action for the last ten years has been essentially 'reductionist' – the elimination of portfolios is favour of 'pure plays', with an intense focus on costs. In essence, energies have been spent undoing the work of the previous 25 years. In 1975 diversified conglomerates accounted for 55 per cent of NYSE value. Now it is approximately 25 per cent.

The break-up of portfolios in favour of pure plays has been endemic. Perhaps the most pervasive single driver has been the concept of core competencies. The academic concept is popularly ascribed to a number of gurus, most notably Gary Hamel of London

Business School.[5] But, in reality, the momentum has come from the capital markets. The proposition is simple – management will inevitably do better at managing something they know well. Focusing on core operating competencies will yield better results than running diverse assets as a portfolio. This would appear to be a move forward – from an extrinsic to an intrinsic source of added value. However, the dominant expression of this strategy is cutting away. It is essentially reductionist and finite in nature.

One classic by-product of the regime of core-competencies is outsourcing – an industry worth around $200 billion and growing at 30 per cent annually! Outsourcing assumes that the activities divested by firms and then outsourced to external suppliers are non-core. The process of reducing the company down to a core of activities assumes that through focused effort these can be performed to world-class standards and that alone will sustain the firm's competitiveness. It is a return to the tenet of specialisation originally articulated by Adam Smith in 1776 – a good sprinter will not make gold in long jump.

The flawless logic tends not to work so perfectly in practice in the context of the firm. Innovation and creativity come from many quarters. But it is a fair bet that in the case of most outsourcing-intensive companies, innovation and creativity will come from outside, not in. The spin-off of Bell Labs (now Lucent) by AT&T, historically the source of so much of that great corporation's innovations, is one blinding example. The explosion of management consulting in the wake of a de-layered middle management is another. The pervasive use of editorial agents by the publishing industry is yet another. All are products of fixed cost reduction exercises that ironically rob the corporation of its energy. R&D is effectively an outsourced function in many contemporary pharmaceutical businesses. The same is true of marketing communications in many fmcg businesses.[6] Even much of the HR management process in many

---

[5] See Hamel, Gary and Prahalad, C.K. *Competing for the Future.* Harvard Business School Press, 1996.

[6] Fast Moving Consumer Goods.

businesses, such as 360° evaluation processing, is outsourced to consulting groups such as Hays or Towers Perrin.

The cult of core competencies appeals to the cleanness of a logic that says when a complex process is pared down to a few basic core pieces, since it is more intelligible, it will do better. The fact that short-term profitability usually goes up as fixed costs are removed tends to reinforce this beguilingly simple, short-term logic. However, as anyone involved in creative processes knows, great things usually come out of a seemingly muddled confluence of diverse influences. Growth and inventiveness are innately complex, untidy processes. The same is true of people and their relationships – of the drivers of a firm's existence. The regime of core competencies tends to miss this trick badly. Reengineering is a reaction to the aggregator strategy and, like any polarity, it fails to see the balanced picture which is reality.

The ultimate in reductionist logic applied to the inner operations of a firm is, of course, 'reengineering'. If the regime of core competencies tends to focus on divestiture of 'non-core' businesses and activities and therefore the structure of the corporation, reengineering focuses on the way work is done or its processes.

This process view of business may seem superficially very different from the structural view of a firm's activity. However, the process and structural viewpoints share something important in common. They both ignore the soul of the company – the beliefs, feelings and commitment of people. Reengineering assumes that a firm is essentially a bundle of mechanical processes, that at heart efficiency is a nuts and bolts process. How very far this misses the point is reflected in the fact that an estimated 85 per cent of reengineering projects are adjudged to leave the firm no better or worse off than before it embarked on the escapade.

There is also an element of paradox to the situation. At the same time as large firms have been shedding assets like there's no tomorrow, those very same firms have been acquiring each other at unprecedented rates. Usually such acquisitions are now within the boundaries of the firm's core competencies, but the irony of chopping with one hand and adding with the other is obvious.

It is in the management of people that the finer shades of the reductionism logic surface. They are surprisingly well disguised and widely misinterpreted. One of the great sound bites of the past ten years has been 'empowerment' – the delegation of operating autonomy to the business unit level. It posits a movement away from control and command management, a liberation of the creative spirit. Not quite so. Empowerment has emerged for a reason. It is not mere coincidence that it has surfaced hand in hand with a period of unprecedented reduction in fixed costs.

Reengineering and its close cousin, downsizing, have been responsible for the elimination of swathes of middle management as traditional hierarchies have been pared away. In the new hollowed-out structures, command and control are no longer practicable – they cannot be policed. Of necessity business unit managers have to be given more discretion. The advent of IT networks has oiled the wheels. Since senior management can now receive, collate and analyse performance statistics on an almost real-time basis from all their business units (or at least they should in principle be able to do so if they have a decent CIO!), they can effectively keep score while apparently delegating management authority – the best of both worlds as far as the corporate staff are concerned. No responsibility but all the power! It may sound unduly cynical, but empowerment is in fact the necessary by-product of headcount reduction. It is not principally an increase in autonomy and 'intrapreneurialism' for its own sake.

Similarly, the increasing use of consultants as substitutes for middle management, along with the increasing use of freelancers, are both driven by the opportunity to move from fixed to variable compensation. Although they are often identified as measures which will allow the firm to tap into individually motivated people, the usual rationale is reduction in committed costs. Again, the focus is on assets and asset structure, not on motivation. Back to our reductionist logic.

The massive shift in the cost base of most large organisations over the past decade has been a necessity to survive in the face of global competition from the East with its lower cost base – and it has done

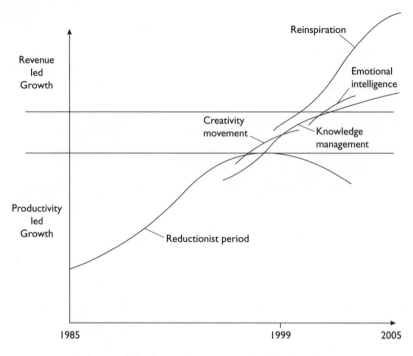

Figure 2.5 The early waves of reinspiration

shareholders proud. But as a strategy it is now approaching exhaustion. In the hollowed-out, empowered organisation, what is left? The wise heads, the collective continuity of middle management are gone. The mentors and visible career paths are swept away. In its place is a swathe of short-term, contracted resource. Many companies risk becoming nothing but a bundle of temporary competencies, without the cultural richness to permit ongoing renewal. What is efficiency one year can quickly turn into atrophy a few years later. A lack of blood supply can only have one result.

This fact has not, of course, passed unnoticed. Business people are mostly smart fellows! In the wake of reengineering there been a resurgence of the clamour to harness creativity. The cries for innovation, for dynamic renewal are the first gropings forward to a new paradigm – the early waves. This is closely bound up with the now universal concept of knowledge as a harnessable and manageable commodity. This in turn owes much of its dynamism to the explosive growth in corporate data networks. More fundamentally, it derives from the fact that cost reduction gains are not a sustainable means of performance renewal. Performance renewal can only come from growth, from actually creating something.

The clamour about creativity, emotional intelligence and knowledge unfortunately often suffers the same weaknesses as the other simplified paradigms we have touched on. You can't restructure your way to creativity. You can't mandate it or simply tell people to be imaginative, to exercise emotional intelligence or to exchange ideas. To the organisation that has been through ten years of reengineering or downsizing (for which reengineering is often a more palatable euphemism), the very idea often seems far-fetched and even insulting. It has the same impersonalised, oversimplified limitation as the core competency debate. It is process- and asset-oriented. It ignores the essential complexity and heterogeneity of genuinely creative environments.

The nomenclature of the knowledge management literature focuses on turning the unowned intellectual contents residing in employees' heads into digital matter which the company owns, which it can leverage, and which the market can supposedly value. It is taking something intangible, residing as a bedfellow with emotions and motivation in the collective head of the workforce, and rendering it tangible – as digits and balance sheet items. Clearly this is not strategy. This is tactics. We will return to this issue in the course of this book.

The drug of short-termism: the shareholder return fixation

Underlying the shift from the aggregator to the reductionist strategy has been the upsurgence of the focus on shareholder value. All quoted organisations – and outside Germany there are comparatively few

YR	0	1	2	3	4	5
CASH FLOW ($m)	100	110	120	130	140	150
DISCOUNT RATE ①	1	1.15^1	1.15^2	1.15^3	1.15^4	1.15^5
DISCOUNT FACTOR	0	1.15	1.32	1.52	1.75	2.01
PERPETUITY ②					$(150 \times 1.05)/0.15)/1.15^5$	
PRESENT VALUE	100	95.7	90.9	85.5	80	597
NET DEBT	200					
NPV	849					

① Assumes discount rate of 15% to reflect risk profile of the business's cash flows
② Assuming 5% growth rate into the future

Figure 2.6 Illustrative calculation of Net Present Value

major organisations which are still in private hands without the intention of at some point coming to market to realise shareholder returns
– are managed to maximise total returns per share.[7] There is clearly
nothing wrong with that goal at all – indeed, any other ultimate
objective would be bizarre. Nor is there anything wrong with the
principle of market valuation.

The market capitalisation of a firm, or the collective value of its
stock, is broadly equivalent to the net present value or NPV of
its future cashflows. For purposes of valuation, cashflows are usually
projected out five years and then a perpetuity value is placed on the
final year which, in turn, is discounted back to its current value. That
is to say, the current value of a firm's stock (its market capitalisation
divided by the number of shares in issue) will be driven by the long-

---

[7] Total shareholder returns are the sum of stock appreciation plus divi-
dends paid out to shareholders.

term, sustainable level of its future cashflows – or at least its anticipated future cashflows. The influence of the current year's performance will be mitigated by expectations concerning its future. It is not
enough for a firm to perform over a year or two. In order to create
real shareholder wealth a firm has to demonstrate it can continue to
grow earnings year after year. It will only do so if its products are
good, it continually innovates and its employees and managers are
committed to driving it forward. A high net present value requires
sustained cashflow that can only be produced by healthy levels
of growth.

What, however, is wrong with the notion of shareholder wealth
is the way it is interpreted by the arbiters of the market – the analysts,
dealers and traders that collectively form the professional decision-
making fabric of the capital markets. While there can be little doubt
that the net present value of a firm will be driven by its long-term
earnings growth, its immediate capitalisation at any one point in time
(and therefore its share price) is usually driven by more short-term
issues. If the firm misses its quarterly earnings target, if it sheds assets
and absorbs an exceptional charge, if a new, unknown competitor
enters and lowers price, if the CEO resigns – all these things will
cause analysts and brokers to take a temporarily different view of a
firm's stock. A simple loss of confidence among this collective group
can be enough to shave a chunk off a firm's value that is very real
to shareholders and to managers whose careers are on the line.

Therefore, while over the long haul share appreciation will be
driven by long-term performance, immediate stock performance does
not necessarily reflect anything more than immediate perceptions. It
does not reflect a firm's 'fundamentals'. This exogenous discrepancy
between short-term perception and longer-term reality is endemic in
today's markets. It is this that drives short-term share performance.
Even large blue-chips regularly experience significant gains and falls
for no intrinsic reasons related to future profit performance. Ironically,
in the case of Internet stocks the logic is entirely flipped. Everyone
believes in the long term and ignores the current losses. This exception only goes to prove the rule!

This short-term volatility would be fine, other than the way it influences managerial decision-making. And there can be no doubt that it does influence senior managers. Most CEOs and group level managers are focused on quarterly earnings figures. A serious dip versus market expectations will result in an immediate reflex. The reason is simple. On a quarterly basis these managers will make a presentation to the markets – to the analysts that follow the stock. The analysts tend to represent banks managing institutional funds. These funds have real power to drive managerial behaviour and they do so with reason. They in turn are dealing in a competitive market. If a fund shows disappointing growth over a year, institutions will switch their money out. The cycle is mutually reinforcing. The fact that both the managers of the firm and the managers of the funds that invest in them are remunerated based on annual shareholder returns, drives the mutually reinforcing cycle even faster.

What are the manifestations of short-termism? What does this really do to the fabric of a company? We have already talked about the focus on costs it induces among management. Annual operating costs can be taken out much more certainly and quickly than revenues can be added. As a result, under quarterly earnings pressure, most firms have focused on costs. Of course, as we have already discussed, cutting costs is a strategy with a finite life.

However, the more insidious manifestation of the behaviour it drives is the treatment of long-term investment. One form of investment is fixed capital – plant and equipment. Accounting rules have evolved over time to mitigate the difficulty of spending now on such 'hard' investments for profits which will only be yielded in the future, through the concept of depreciation. Depreciation allows the cost of investment to be amortised over notionally the same period it will yield offsetting profits for the business. The same is not, however, true of that other area of long-term investment – training people.

Training is probably the most powerful tool in a company's armoury in upgrading its capability to compete – just as education is almost certainly the most significant driver of a country's long-term competitiveness. It is also one of the principal methods of ensuring that its people share a common sense of purpose and vision.

Training has always figured highly in the development and sustenance of the world's great social institutions. Education not only leads to an accumulation of knowledge. It also embeds a philosophy which drives the collective view of the world shared by that particular group. Education is far more powerful that indoctrination, far more powerful than propaganda, far more powerful than edicts. It internalises a way of thinking which becomes inseparable from the nature of the individual. This is why, as we will come to see, the great religions place such store in the continual process of learning, why the Buddhist traditionally devotes three hours out of every day to religious study.

Driven by short-term EPS targets, most corporations by contrast have let spend on education wither on the vine. The average spend on training as a percentage of revenue has fallen from 2 per cent in 1970 to 0.3 per cent today, roughly equivalent to the investment most firms make in office stationery such as paperclips and marker pens! The reason is simple – that the costs of education hit the bottom line today for perceived uncertain benefits in the future. If there is a level of employee churn, then the perception is that money has been thrown away. Earnings are dented.

The management-level educational process has effectively been outsourced by the corporate world to the MBA institutions. This has the positive effect of removing it as a fixed cost from the company P&L. However, it does so at the cost of developing a cohesive sense of shared ethos and purpose unique to the firm. The average MBA churns through at least two jobs in their first five years out of school. In relying on them for future management, firms risk seriously eroding their basis of differentiation.

A third key manifestation of short-termism is the lack of investment in organic renewal by most firms. Even with the offsetting cushion of depreciation, investment in new business lines, or in starting new businesses altogether has a current cost which will only be offset by earnings in the future. By contrast, acquisitions, if made at competitive pricing levels, will typically contribute immediate earnings per share. The offsetting amortisation of goodwill, reflecting the cost of the investment, has until recently been avoidable through pooling in the US (although this is now disappearing), an annual revaluation of goodwill in the UK or by being stretched over a period which exceeds the multiple of after-tax earnings paid for the target.[8] The markets are now increasingly turning to after-tax EBITDA[9] as a measure of performance which again avoids goodwill amortisation effects in terms of driving the valuation of the acquirer and therefore makes acquired earnings essentially 'free'. Not surprisingly, acquisitions have become vastly favoured over internal start-ups by most quoted firms.

Organic growth through indigenous start-ups plus fill-in acquisitions is a vital way for a corporation to achieve continual renewal. Identity and culture tends to be preserved, although in new, innovative forms. Home-grown talent is given a new palette on which to achieve expression of the company's core capabilities.

The process of acquisition is a very different one. If the target is small, it will typically lose its own identity as it is assimilated. The process of assimilation can be accommodated if the business is relatively small without disrupting the social continuity of the acquirer. However, this is not the case with the big industrial and service sector mergers that are sweeping the corporate landscape. Interestingly, the focus in such transactions is usually on ensuring that the client facing brands are preserved. What is often not preserved is the corporate identity. The volume of name changes at the corporate level over the past decade has never been greater. Name changes are a proxy for changes in the context, meaning and continuity of the work environment for that other set of customers – employees. The loss of identity and social cohesion in the wake of major deals certainly

---

[8] If acquired annual earnings exceed the annualised accounting cost of buying those earnings or the goodwill depreciation, the deal will add incremental earnings at no cost.

[9] After tax EBITDA is increasingly known as EBIADAT (earnings before interest, amortisation, depreciation, after tax).

influences the widespread failure of 'deal'-driven growth to deliver superior shareholder returns.

A fourth regular manifestation of short-termism is the nature of competition itself. The central quality of a powerful community is that it is driven by its own logic, by a sense of what it is and what objectives it holds as important. In essence, it creates a unique set of parameters against which to measure its success. It sets its own objectives, whether focused on product innovation or great service, the ultimate fruit of which is shareholder wealth.

The modern corporation tends not to take this intrinsic view of its destiny. Increasingly, firms measure themselves solely against their competitors rather than against original internal goals. One of the most pervasive use of consultants is for purposes of benchmarking. Benchmarking typically sets uniform parameters across businesses. It propagates an inexorable process of emulation – like some beach beauty contest! It makes great business for consultants but the result is gravitation towards sameness.

It should not therefore be surprising that most businesses competing closely in a given sector look increasingly alike. Employees will regularly shift between them. Clients will find it hard to tell between them. What after all really distinguishes the Big Five accountancy groups or the bulge-bracket investment banks? Many of their employees will have worked in at least one of the competitor firms. Benchmarking will tend to establish uniform short-term goals across a sector and these will be tracked by the market. Every shift in yield, churn, margin, EPS, etc., will be closely followed by the analysts. In a world moving towards homogeneity, the ones that will win will be those firms that buck the trend!

So what? Short-term returns are real returns!

So, if short-termism is structural, driven by market dynamics, what problem does it really pose? Are firms really at risk? The answer is they have never been more so. In the 1870s many firms stuck to manual assembly and ignored mechanised manufacturing. In the 1970s as many firms were slow to adopt computerisation. Few of them are around today. How many firms you know well are ignoring the need to build emotional commitment among their internal communities? Probably many. They've survived Y2K, but these firms will probably not be around in 20 years.

How loyal do most larger corporations feel to their employees? What sense of obligation do they feel to their emotional welfare? Not much. This is, of course, fine if the costs of knowledge migration are low. Hence, the metal bashing business could afford to risk a rupture of the social bond with low-skilled workers. The only check on the natural inclination to continually reduce social obligation (and with it costs), were unions. In most developed economies, if not yet extinct, unions are going that way.

But life is not that simple anymore. Most successful businesses increasingly derive their competitive advantage from the knowledge base and emotional drive of their employees. Whether it be the process management experts in a steel mill or the insolvency consultants in a Big Five professional services firm, there has been a dramatic shift of value out of the fixed asset and capital base of most companies and into the heads of its skilled employees. The IT-driven knowledge economy means that much of the value added of the modern corporation walks out of the door at night. No one has successfully put a number on it, but human capital probably outweighs fixed and financial capital by five to one in terms of contribution to market value. Just it doesn't appear on the balance sheet.

In this situation, the contract between the firm and the employee suddenly takes on new meaning as a driver of the competitiveness of the firm. The annual churn rates which never really worried the top management group in the past, should now be an issue of intense concern. The skilled employee can ostensibly migrate between temporary ports of call or employment nodes. If enough of them decide to shift to another node or, indeed, as so often happens, to start up on their own, a firm can suffer a sudden and dramatic loss of competitive advantage. It is no longer of advantage to the firm to jeopardise the sense of mutual social obligation. The benefits of reducing fixed employee costs and the flexibility of outsourcing are usually far outweighed by the risk of the firm's tacit know-how migrating away because of mutual indifference.

A tired chestnut: the culture and values debate

On an intellectual level at least, we have hopefully created some consensus that the cohesiveness and robustness of the identification between employees and their firm are a major source of competitive advantage. At a time where product and technologically-driven differentiation tends to be fleeting, the only locus that makes one firm different from another is its 'firmness'.

The question is what is 'firmness'? We can see the intense commitment to intellectual integrity of a McKinsey; we can see the semi-devotional drive of a Goldman Sachs; the innovative compulsiveness of an Intel. But how can the idea be pinned down into something useful? A tool? A framework? Unless it can be rendered specific it has no hope in hell of superseding the structural and process paradigms that dog contemporary management thinking.

The two terms commonly used to encapsulate this ethereal, elusive concept are 'culture' and 'values'. These two terms are now becoming the staple fare of management books. Consulting firms have begun to focus on diagnosing their clients' core values and identity firms earn big fees helping clients communicate these values internally.

There is no doubt that culture exists as a phenomenon, and that certain values tend to underpin it. The issue is, can a culture be created? Can values be inseminated? In short, is there anything in the observation about culture and values that gives management a tool to shape a corporation's success? To guide its people? Does writing them down and despatching them to every employee get you anywhere? Does repeating them again and again *ad nauseam* create value?

Culture and values are not so much a tool or doctrine which can be used by management as the articulation of an idea. At the risk of infuriating some heavy-weight business thinkers, this idea is as abstract as talking about the meaning of life. If we breathe, we exist; if a society exists, it will have a culture and values. The term culture is also hopelessly imprecise, describing a bundle of diverse constituent parts that are impossible to unravel. This level of abstraction and imprecision inevitably leads to frustration on the part of managers looking for practical ways forward.

Of course, the frustration with the slippery, elusiveness of the concept is also part of its potential strength. Those tools which are perennially created by management gurus and which can be tactically deployed by managers to extract short-term gain are not typically the tools that will lead to long-term success. One good thing about the concept of culture is that it evolves over time and, while a single CEO can have an impact on it, unless they take surgical action they will not fundamentally reconstitute it during their tenure, except perhaps through merger or acquisition. In a time of re-invention and continual churning of paradigms this means there cannot be so much manipulation.

However, in terms of positively enhancing the competitiveness of a firm, the exhortation that culture is the key does not help. Nor does the focus on values. Listing them or representing them as a colour or picture, as do a number of reputable consulting firms, is almost hilariously childish. The focus is sort of in the right place but the viewing lens has to be magnified and intensified. So what is the answer? This brings us back to the reinspiration model.

Summary

Poised on the next wave of change and the dawn of a new millennium, the question is, where does the reengineering, merger and outsourcing-weary corporation go from here? Corporate reinspiration posits a counter force – the re-assembly of the corporation. It is not about vertical integration or portfolios. It is not about bringing functions back in house. It is not turning the clock back. It is a positive step forward. It is about re-establishing the contract between employees and the firm. It is about restoring the collection of beliefs, approaches, practices and character that make the successful corporation unique, that drive its differentiation. It offers a route to innovation and creativity. Above all, adopting the reinspiration model requires that we, management, change the way we think about competitiveness. That we shift mind-sets. The first step in that direction is to understand more of the origins of reinspiration.

3

The origins of the seven
well-trodden paths to reinspiration

The lessons of the great religious
movements

The reinspiration model is founded on the seven rules or paths (meaning they are to be learned, not mandated) we have already touched on. You may be healthily sceptical at this point in the journey. Are they really the ultimate source of long-term competitive advantage for great organisations? Who says so? What is the evidence or is this just some more mumbo-jumbo management BS? The answer is emphatically no. The proof? The great religions have all the proof we should need. The issue is how to apply the irrefutable lessons they offer.

This chapter will deal with the proof. The next eight chapters will deal with the application. Let's run along the seven paths one at a time. But one caveat before we start; the seven great religions each have voluminous texts with vastly different interpretations of what constitutes the religious life. Working through them in detail and consecutively would consume many more pages than this book can accommodate (and this is a book about business not religion!). Instead we have crystallised the key insights which are common

to them all, from Christianity, Hinduism, Buddhism, Zionism, Confucianism, Taoism to Islam, and summarised them in a form that is
of utility more than of academic integrity. If such simplification and
distillation offend anyone, they have our full apologies and we beg
their patience.

The seven seminal paths

Path 1 They provide a context of moral authority and a framework which offers personal redemption

All the religions promulgate a view of what constitutes good
morality. The term 'moral authority' sounds like some schoolmasterly
dictum – anachronistic and outdated. This stuffiness is not in fact
the way the religions look at it. The attitude the great religions take
to moral authority is that we each have to be shown the path to self-
betterment. It is the duty of religion to illuminate the path, to furnish
a framework through which the individual can progress to fulfilment
of their potential for good.

All the great religions, having identified the obstacles in our path,
provide a framework, a methodology for redemption. The process of
working through the framework, following the path, constitutes the
internalisation of a moral code – a self-training course administered
along closely defined lines. Like any professional environment, religion provides a ladder for emotional and spiritual fulfilment, a means
to achieve moral endorsement – a fundamental need for any self-
respecting person.

Take Hinduism for example – a religion that underpins the lives
of a billion human beings. Hinduism is an ethic which says that
everyone gets what they deserve and that choices are the key determinants of destiny. Hinduism, however, provides a framework to help
its disciples achieve this destiny called Yoga. Yoga is a method of
training designed to lead to integration with the meaning that lies
in the inner recesses of all of us. Yoga promulgates four paths: the

reflective path through knowledge or Juana Yoga; the path that guides through love or Bhakti Yoga; the path marked out by work or Karma Yoga; and finally the experimental path, Raja Yoga. No one path is correct and according to the stage in life in which a person finds themselves, one path will be more appropriate than another. Hinduism is very tolerant of complexity, human differences and parallel alternatives, taking the view that the various religions are all alternative paths to the same goal. But it is clear in providing its own method of achieving moral fulfilment.

Buddhism, the Puritan reaction to a decadent Hinduism of the fourth century AD, promulgates its own model of redemption from the strangulating hernia of the ego and separateness. This is through the Eightfold Path – right views, right intent; right speech; right conduct; right livelihood; right effort; right mindfulness; and right concentration. The ultimate goal, Nirvana, is a state of liberation from the constraints of the ego and ambition. In contrast to the image of a drug-induced state this may conjure up in the mind of Western folk brought up on the Beatles, the process of moral fulfilment is dominantly one of learning. Buddhism sees ignorance and not sin as the offender, concurring with Spinoza that 'to understand something is to be delivered of it'. It recognises the danger run by most people of mistaking life's means, the daily process of earning a crust, as life's end. The Eightfold Path is its framework for delivery from this fate. It provides a means to avoid slipping into the mire of endless self-preoccupation.

Confucianism, which lays claim to the souls of more than 20 per cent of the world's population, has a far less abstracted model of self-improvement, typical of its preoccupation with social rectitude. It focuses on the cultivation of the social self. Its framework of self-betterment is best termed 'patterns of prestige', comprising 'Jen' or human heartedness; 'Chun Tzu' or the perfect hostess; 'Li' or *savoir faire* and 'Te', the spontaneous consent that comes from good leadership. The cultivation of these social qualities is based on a conviction that it is the inculcation of harmonious social relationships that drives the success of a country – a sense that the most admired state will be that which develops the most exalted culture, the noblest philosophy, the finest art; the highest 'wen'.[1] Confucianism's moral framework is one of endless self improvement in order to fulfil one's social obligations ever more fully. In this respect Confucianism's moral framework is much more akin to the philosophy of a social institution than an obviously spiritual one.

Islam, like Confucianism, is perhaps less accommodating of duality and alternatives than Hinduism and Buddhism. Its moral framework is somewhat more prescriptive, focused on following the straight path. There are no viable alternative routes. The 'Five Pillars' govern the private life of Muslims in their dealings with God – the Shahadah, the confession of faith; the canonical prayer to be constant; charity; the observation of Ramadan; and pilgrimage. Islam, of all the great religions, spans the most highly dispersed set of cultures and geography, through from the Middle East to South East Asia. The five pillars bind together these scattered peoples, ensuring that they share a strict creed that transcends loyalty to nations and ethnic groups. It is not a framework with easy compromises. In this respect it shares something with Judaism and its progeny, Christianity. It differs from Hinduism and Buddhism pointedly in this regard.

Both Judaism and Christianity share the same moral framework for guiding people to self-betterment – the Ten Commandments. The Commandments stand as the moral foundation of the Western world, familiar to every reader of this book, binding virtually all of us in the West to a common set of values. Whether we formally choose to conform to them or not, they set a benchmark for behaviour which is pervasive and internalised, even if the Church as an institution has taken a serious popularity beating (and more and more churches are metamorphosing into pubs and night-clubs!).

---

[1] Wen means a high level of cultural and social sophistication among a community, where the basic requirements of order, stability and economic well-being have been achieved and superseded by higher cultural goals of expression of complex ideas and philosophical truths.

The existence of such frameworks to govern the process of self-improvement responds to the profound need all people share to have a methodology, a model by which they can govern themselves, reference to which provides meaning, security, purpose and which also provides an index of achievement and standing. Above all, it is the yardstick of recognition and status – a fundamental human need.

Most businesses, by contrast, share a trivial set of universal behavioural mores. Most executives would not survive long without a tie; hand shaking is the *de facto* norm, even in Japan; sex at work will not usually do. But clearly these characteristics do not represent a substantive moral framework. In most businesses there is the glaring absence of any substantive aspirational framework. Some companies document codes of behaviour or articulate values. Some even go so far as to employ consulting firms to enshrine these in mission statements, embody them in corporate colours or disseminate them as glossy magazines. The average mission statement is an infamous vacuity (one notable exception perhaps being the oft quoted credo of Johnson and Johnson). Their value as a moral framework that provides meaning to employees is, as we will explore more fully, truly limited indeed.

Unifying behavioural characteristics do emerge in most good firms, usually as a result of years of self-selection in the recruiting process. These condition what is understood to be the way to do things and provide a yardstick for advancement. McKinsey people all seem to share certain qualities; Arthur Andersen seems to attract a type. But even here, it is hard to discern a credo, a moral framework which fulfils the collective emotional needs of the firm.

How powerful it would be for a global firm to have a shared credo, a moral framework as meaningful to its employees as the creed of Confucius or Buddha! How extraordinarily distinctive it would become; how effectively it would differentiate itself! Why? Because it would fulfil a fundamental human need common to its employees in a proprietorial fashion that was competitively defensible.

Path 2 They emphasise looking beyond individual concerns and the primacy of integration or surrender

The importance of moving beyond personal concerns and an egocentric view of progress towards a collective, 'de-personalised' view of the world is common to all the great religions, although in different degrees. Obsessive personalisation is seen as intensely limiting to development. It is also seen as corrosive to personal well-being. Success is to be achieved with others and through others. The great religions are fundamentally social is this regard. They are also somewhat at odds with the pervasive contemporary ethic of personal, individual competitiveness – the cult religion of a Michael Jordan or Madonna.

Probably at one end of the spectrum on the anti-ego trail is Hinduism. Hinduism regards the centring of meaning on the self as far too limiting. As a religion it is preoccupied with the search for the larger whole to relieve life of its triviality. Religion becomes a quest for meaning beyond self-centredness. Hinduism does not posit that such a tall demand will be appropriate for all people. True to form, it is accommodating of parallel paths. Some men and women will play out the game of personal desire, or self-fulfilment, with absolute zest and never get beyond it. Chasing sexual gratification and cash will preoccupy them all of their days. Hinduism does not say this is bad and does not demand its suppression – indeed, it acknowledges that trying to suppress it will be like trying to quench a fire by pouring butane on it. It does, however, suggest that for intelligent people this game will prove limiting, that ultimately the competitive exclusion it involves will prove precarious, the fruits unfulfilling. This also holds true when the individual matures and when the 'game' takes on its more social manifestation of a pursuit for fame and power. As Plato put it in a different way, 'Poverty consists not in the decrease of one's possessions but in the increase of one's greed.'

If self-gratification is limiting, what do we really want out of life? What are our higher, more fundamental goals? Hinduism posits that we want to see ourselves as part of the future, that none of us can bear seeing a future of which we are not a part. We also want to discover the meaning of what we are doing, to satiate our curiosity. Finally we want joy, a release from frustration and boredom or, as Proust termed it, *Ennui*. We want release from childish self-identification with inconsequential events. Overall, Hinduism posits that what we really desire is release from finitude; the finitude that restricts us having access to limitless being, consciousness and joy. It says that the only thing stopping us getting there is our individual ego. Only when the ego is put aside can we be liberated and get in touch with our Brahman or Atman. Of course, this is anathema to a decade devoted to ego. Mahatma Gandhi is remembered by most Westerners as a hero of an eponymous movie, not for his message of selflessness.

The same theme of release is echoed in the other great religions. In Christianity the release from the confines of the ego is achieved via love – love for one's fellow men and women. Eastern Orthodoxy in particular stresses the importance of surrender to a collective interest in order to achieve salvation – one can be damned alone but only saved by others.

Part of the process of abnegating the self involves the linking with a larger whole, a collective interest beyond the self. Religion in general focuses on this issue of at-one-ness, re-binding, or, in its Greek root, re-ligio. This conviction finds its most extreme expression in the primal religions[2] which reflect the belief that human beings and nature belong to a single order; that everything visible is bound together in a single spirit. Since the idea of union, of oneness, finds its roots in the primordial beginnings of religion, it is easy to understand why it has become such a core tenet of modern religious life, down to the Sufis of Islam who go so far as to abhor the separation from God implied by self-consciousness. Buddhism, in particular, sees separateness and the desire for private fulfilment, all those

---

[2] Perhaps the most cohesive remaining of the primal religions is that of the Australian Aboriginals, followed by the Hopi, Navaho and other North American cultures.

inclinations which tend to continue or increase separateness, as the key to human suffering. Or as Ibsen eloquently put it in his depiction of a lunatic asylum where 'each shuts himself in a cask of self, the cask stopped with a bung of self and seasoned in a well of self.'

None of this, importantly, abnegates personal responsibility. One of Islam's tenets is that 'whoever gets to himself a sin gets it solely on his own responsibility'.[3] In the case of Confucianism, as we have discussed, the individual is committed to a project of never-ending self-cultivation. Authority is not automatic, it must be earned. The self is nothing more than the centre of relationships. It is constructed through its interactions with others and is defined by the sum of its social roles.

Central to the concept of union, the opposite of separateness, is the idea of surrender – surrender to greater goals than those achievable by personal, muscular, egotistical exertion. As William James put it, 'In those states of mind which fall short of religion, surrender is submitted to as an imposition of necessity and the sacrifice in undergone at the very best without complaint. In the religious life, on the contrary, surrender and sacrifice are positively espoused'.[4] The idea of surrender is, of course, largely viewed as unpalatable to the West. It is closely identified with weakness and faintheartedness.

The West is importantly driven by Protestantism which tends more than the other great religions to promote individualism. The US in particular, driven by Protestant sentiment, has laid an acute emphasis on individual improvement and personal enlightenment through private education, sparked by the Jeffersonian Enlightenment. Individualism, once it has appeared, tends to be contagious and spreads like an epidemic. The question asked by the majority of the great religions is, does the conscious tempering of the urge to individualism provide a more compelling environment in which to nurture productivity and collective performance or should we all simply fight it out?

---

3   See Fritzjof, Schuon. *Understanding Islam*. Penguin, 1972.
4   See James, William. *The Varieties of Religious Experience*. Macmillan, 1961.

The idea of 'selflessness' is clearly very contentious within the context of the corporation. Most modern management systems stress individual performance and promote individuality. Remuneration systems are dominantly based on personal performance. There is a general drive for individual accountability which the advent of IT networks has facilitated enormously. We all know the big CEOs. We are all as shareholders prepared to reward them vastly as individuals. We are fundamentally geared to competitive isolationism even if it is emotionally uncomfortable and, at the extreme, dysfunctional.

This has, however, been recognised to have its limitations even by the most individualistic management teams. One person partner-ships do not get the firm where it needs to go. One response has been the widespread adoption of team concepts, whereby groups of people are incentivised to win together. These often utilise 360° evaluation methods. Teams are drawn from different departments or reflect the heterogeneity of the firm. Such cross-functional team struc-tures are often the result of reengineering exercises, designed with the intention of streamlining internal transactions.

Ironically, however, in many organisations teams simply act to increase the degree of organisational separation between groups of people. Teams rarely function effectively with more than about 14 members. A firm that has turned to teams can find itself composed of dozens of warring tribes. At their worst, they tend to encourage desegregation, not re-integration. The corporation becomes cellular. It loses the power of its wholeness.

What is wrong with individual competition within a firm? Individualism, after all, tends to deliver short-term results. If 50 people have a week in which ten of them can earn 10 000 bucks they will fight a lot harder to get there. However, they may not co-operate to build something that will last 50 years. Reflect for a moment on the example of Chartres where few people were even paid. Should they have instituted a regimen of daily slab-shifting counts? Would that have produced a better result, more efficiently?

The promotion of success through internal competitiveness is so deeply ingrained in contemporary management norms that it is not

even considered an issue. What we do know from institutional examples of longevity, however, is that shared motives, common goals that
tend towards a de-emphasis of individualism, that inspire identification with non-personal objectives, lead to greater long-term success.
Something is very rotten in the State of Denmark. It is an important issue we will return to in detail presently.

Path 3 *They are characterised by deeply ingrained ritual and use of symbolism*

Ritual is a vital ingredient of the human state of happiness. Nothing
else can take its place. Knowing we will do the same thing today as
we did yesterday and the day before gives us fundamental reassurance
about our continuity. That is why we all cherish our favourite pubs,
our favourite chairs, our favourite socks; why we tend to take the
same route to work everyday. Furthermore, knowing that the same
actions have rewarded like-minded people in the past is confirmation
of our judgement. Life itself is a ritualised event, from the ceremonies
surrounding death and birth to the way we behave with others. Ritual
is at the heart of our beginnings.

The great religions have taken the seminal need for ritual and
turned it into a set of fundamental markers governing spiritual life
through from the ceremonial days that mark the calendar, each with
its own processions, to the ritualised gestures and patterns of behaviour which make religious events religious. Even for relative agnostics,
rituals such as Christmas, Easter or Ramadan underpin our family lives.

Perhaps the most powerful expression of ritual is through symbols.
Most people find it very difficult to conceive much less be motivated
by anything that is very far removed from direct experience. Religion
naturally gives rise to symbols as the mind tries to think about invisible, abstract ideas of morality and purpose. Symbols are used to
denote complex meaning without requiring a detailed revisiting and
re-inventing of the idea each time. Symbols are the foundation of
any way of thinking, religious or otherwise.

For the primal religions there is no need for symbols. The primal religions (the most notable being that practised by the Australian Aboriginals) do not have any symbolic structures. There is a direct link between matter and its spiritual root. Every object is a reflection of a superior reality which contains the physical reality. As a consequence, among American Indians there is no word for art. There are no allegories. Ritual alone is enough, whether expressed through wild dancing or meditation.

For modern man, however, symbols are vital. Symbols crystallise an idea in the immediate senses. We are surrounded by them. They are the mental landmarks defining the landscape of our lives. Life without them is inconceivable. We would have no way of finding our way through the vast weight of information and stimuli. Imagine finding a rest-room without the symbol of a man or woman to guide us!

The great religions adopt symbols as a seminal language that cross all geographies. Taoism, like Buddhism, is probably best recognised by its symbols; the yin yan disks in Tokyo temples, its grotesque figurines, its ceremonial drums. Christianity is universally invoked by the cross, Zionism by the five-pointed star, Islam by the star and sickle moon. Symbols and ritual are the real-life underpinnings of these institutions. They are what bring them alive.

Not all the great religions have the same level of comfort with symbols. Symbols, being powerful motivators, can be deceptive and divisive. As Milton put it in 'Paradise Lost', 'Satan's image betrayed the truth . . .'.[5] Protestantism, rather like Buddhism before it, prefers freedom of thought to the security of symbols. It repudiates the 'little piece of form'. It holds the view that all human manifestations are imperfect, everything must point beyond itself to God. Similarly, Buddhism rejects words as a distraction, concerned that you can believe in the words without believing in the concept they reflect. (Sound familiar?) Zen goes further and rejects scriptures and creeds altogether, *'signposts are not the destination, maps are not the terrain.'*

---

[5] See Milton, John, 'Paradise Lost'.

Instead it proposes the Koan – a riddle 'like an alarm clock it is set to awaken the mind from its dream of rationality.'[6] Similarly, Taoism rejects the ritualised, symbolised observance of Confucianism which it sees as brittle and prone to break.

Whatever their level of comfort with symbolism, all the great religions share fundamentally symbolic languages. Each great religion has its text; Hinduism the Vedas; Confucianism the Classics; Judaism the Torah; Christianity the Bible and Islam the Koran. As well as imparting knowledge, each text also functions as a symbol of higher truths. At one extreme the Koran is not even historical but directly doctrinal. It is not about the truth; it is the truth. Symbol and symbolised converge. But all the texts share this quality to a degree. They are not a ripping yarn. They are symbols of faith and the qualities that faith embodies.

The business world has begun more recently to awaken to the extraordinary power of ritual and symbolism to foster a strong collective identity. It has even spawned an industry called Corporate Identity Design. At the conventional end, this revolves around the ubiquitous corporate logo and glossy, high resolution literature. The budgets to put these programmes in place can sometimes be truly mind-boggling. British Telecom's facelift in the early 1990s was rumoured to have run up a bill of £150 million, AT&T's revamp at the same period probably cost around the same, although, it must be stated clearly, both firms have in the process been through absolute consumer-driven revolutions that have transformed their competitiveness.

Identity programmes usually, however, fall well short of symbolism. The big difference between most corporate identity programmes and the symbolist ritual of the great religions is the difference between form and content. Religious symbolism serves a purpose. Like words, it is a route to a truth which is complex to explain but which can be more readily and universally accessed through symbols. Anyone seeing a crucifix knows both what literally happened to a fellow called

---

[6] See Smith, Huston, *The World's Religions*. Harper Collins, 1991.

Jesus of Nazareth but, more profoundly, the set values from which that event is inseparable.

The same cannot be said of many corporate identity programmes. A corporate logo does not typically give rise to a set of values. It does not invoke a code of behaviour. It simply denotes a brand. A brand is very different from an icon or symbol. It connotes certain values of consumption, of group or individual endorsement. It does not connote a set of profoundly held beliefs. A good corporate logo does not mean to an employee what a consumer brand means to a punter. The level and complexity of involvement are fundamentally different between a place where one spends the bulk of one's day versus a chocolate bar or vacuum cleaner or even a car.

The fact that an identity programme is usually a one-time discrete revamp, often contracted out to a few-person consultancy, says a lot about the degree of genuine identification between the brand identity and the company. This is a vast opportunity missed by most firms. Without indigenous symbols they have no proprietary language. We will have a lot to say about language presently.

Path 4 They are founded on well-understood tradition

All the great religions are founded on a keen sense of tradition. They are built on the well-trodden stones of what has gone before. They respond to the fact that we all have a profound psychological need to feel we have an origin which endorses our present, that we all like to think well of our antecedents. It is part of a healthy self-image.

Of the great religions, Judaism is perhaps the most deeply wedded to tradition. In contrast to the abstraction of the Greeks which has so influenced the West, Judaism is not founded on an idea but an event. Judaism takes the view that the historical context in which life is lived affects one's existence in every way, delineating its problems and its opportunities. All the historical religions – Christianity,

Judaism, Islam – which are founded on a concrete event, not a principle, share this same viewpoint. A sense of origin is vital. Unlike Hinduism where destiny lies outside history altogether, Judaism proposes collective, accumulating action through the generations.

Confucianism is similarly steeped in respect for tradition. Confucius asserted the importance of tradition as a counter-thrust to the corrosive loss of social order in the China of his day. It was also a rejection of the realist option of compelling people to behave properly through force – the same realism later espoused by Hobbes who famously envisioned a life where man was left to his devices as 'nasty, brutish and above all short'.[7] Confucianism involved a shift from spontaneous to deliberate tradition through the 'patterns of prestige' we have already discussed. It was artificial, engineered, but it worked. It brought with it a reverence of wisdom and old age increasingly alien to the contemporary culture of the West.

The West, and particularly the US, has proposed reason as an alternative to tradition – the Jeffersonian belief that once educated and informed, citizens can be relied upon to behave sensibly. The absence of tradition in the US, the lack of a historical example and the paucity of cultural rootedness amongst certain deracinated groups, have undoubtedly contributed to its high level of social turbulence. In the face of the limits of what the Jeffersonian ideal has been able to deliver, it has been forced to counter this with force – the Hobbsian approach of a strong CIA, tough cops, crowded jails and the rule of the handgun enshrined by the NRA.

Few corporations have a well-honed base of traditions. As few last more than 50 years that should hardly be surprising! In the absence of a keen sense of tradition, of powerful patterns of behaviour, most corporations resort to a mixture of carrot and stick. Certain behaviour patterns are enforced through individual incentives and certain through punishments. The question is, does the absence of tradition, even if as in the case of Confucianism it might be a manufactured tradition, constitute the loss of a good trick? The answer is yes.

---

7   See Hobbes, Thomas, *The Leviathan*. Penguin, 1986.

Tradition has the benefit of providing a framework to guide behaviour without stifling it. It empowers but directs individual energies. It gives something worth fighting to preserve and propagate. It is the invisible hand. That role is not the monopoly of the demand and supply curve.

Of course, the concept of tradition is a difficult one in the Internet age where everything is being invented and revolutionised at such a pace, where there appear to be no precedents for what is going to happen next. The term 'tradition' is unfortunately associated with conservatism, defence of the status quo, institutionalisation. Tradition in its true sense denotes a stable platform, guaranteeing enough continuity to allow healthy risk taking and individual endeavour. A level of security and confidence is a precursor to successful innovation and risk taking. The bold entrepreneurs who drag themselves out of deprivation are often quoted but constitute a small minority. The idea that it takes the threat of absolute ruin to spur someone to great acts is the stuff of schoolbook heroes. For most over-achievers to goad themselves to bold deeds and great inventions, basic insecurities usually have to be overcome first – a stable family situation, a mortgage under control, a identity of which they can be proud. Likewise, companies rarely make good gambles when their backs are against the wall – the focus on stripping out costs takes firm hold.

Continuity also tends to nurture innovation on the foundation of inherited skill sets, through an accumulation of expertise. The Swiss in banking and precision engineering, the Italians in design, the British in the professions are all innovators in their fields because of continuity. Their leadership is founded on clusters of skills, bred and refined through tradition. As such, they can justify the market premium for their products and services. The question for most firms who have a heritage is how to keep it alive, evolving and relevant. For those that lack it, the challenge is how to invent it.

*Path 5 They are essentially optimistic in
their outlook; their view of the competitive universe
is positive*

> 'In its broadest sense, religion says that there is an
> unseen order and that our supreme good lies in rightful
> relation to it.' (William James)

All the great religions assure us that if we could see the full picture
we would find it more integrated, more wonderful than we suppose.
This vision of a beatific order, slightly beyond the grasp of our compre-
hension, inspired the Elysian landscapes of Giotto, the aerial frescos
of Michaelangelo. It has made people over the centuries stretch their
intellects to reach new heights. If things are pervaded by a grand
design, they are not only more integrated, they are also better than
they seem. There lies in this assurance the hope of a better personal
state worth fighting for – a redemption. Redemption is the principal
goal of all the great religions; the movement towards a better, a
happier state of being.

Perhaps the most forward-thrusting religion of them all is Judaism.
Despite Canaan being less than the size of a US State, it has left its
profound mark on Western civilisation. Unlike its contemporary
forces – Egypt, Assyria, Phoenicia – which buttressed the status quo,
Judaism was a reforming impetus, driven by the conviction that things
were not as they should be. It resisted the notion that the current
power arrangements were the all important determinants of one's position in life. Had it not, it would have plunged its people into despair.
Instead it began an expectant search for meaning, for a better lot. It
took the view that, unlike the Greek and Roman gods, 'Yahweh' was
there to lift his people out of slavery – that all aspects of the world
were pervaded by meaning and purpose waiting to be discovered.
Judaism tends to assume that the fault originated from ourselves and
not from the stars. Hence it demands a creative response.

Buddhism shares Judaism's invocation to positive action. Buddhism was a reaction to the fatalism of the Brahministic interpretation

of Hinduism which suggested it would take thousands of incarnations for a low caste member to gain release as a Brahmin. In its place it posited a creed of self-reliance and self-formation. Again, it affirmed a positive objective, a route to salvation. Christianity, Confucianism and Islam all share a similar ethos – that achieving salvation requires a personal act of will. It is not fated, predestined. The great religions stand counter-point to the tragic fatalism of the Greeks. Our role is there for us to make and it is our moral duty to forge the right path.

Most corporations are 'expectant'. Their principal instinct is to drive towards improvement, towards a better lot. However, that sentiment is all too often only relevant to the members of the Board and a relatively small number of senior managers, all of whom will have the acute incentive of seeing the stock price rise. For this group of people the fruits of positivism are very sweet! By contrast, most normal employees have increasingly focused on what they might lose through change, whether through restructuring or downsizing. Their frame of reference is negative. The status quo is good. Intrapreneurship might sound good but it is anathema to most when the dominant frame of mind is 'Oh shit, what the hell do I do about the college fees?'.

The creation of an optimistic frame of mind is rarely a conscious policy among large corporations. The atmosphere of euphoric expectation in smaller entrepreneurial firms, where everyone shares in the excitement, is partly why they usually experience more impressive growth rates. Most large firms can only look on with a mixture of contempt and envy at the messianic motivation of the upstarts snapping at their heals. The explosive growth of the Microsofts, Amazons and Dells should have taught the behemoths that positive, optimistic enthusiasm is an important driver of competitiveness. The issue is how to turn that observation into a positive strategy for firms which are not being electrified by the exhilarating vertigo of explosive growth.

Path 6 They encourage the asking of the big questions

There are three big questions which have always divided people as long as there have been people:

1 Is our destiny in our own hands or dictated by forces beyond our control? Is there some grand, immutable plan with an inevitability called fate? Or is fate something we invent for ourselves?
2 Is the universe friendly or hostile? Is God really there to save us or are we just gnats in some random, Darwinist bio-game?
3 Is head or heart best? Should we do what is best for us or society in the most dispassionate way or should we follow our feelings and urges? Passion or precision?

These same questions have divided the great religions themselves. Hinduism has its Buddhism; Buddhism, in turn, has divided into Theravada versus Mahayanista; Confucianism has its Taoism; Catholicism its Protestantism. Each circles around the other, vying over these questions.

Has this damaged them organisationally? Would it have been better that such questions were suppressed if they were going to produce schism, to compromise their unitarianism? The answer is probably no. The process of enquiry has in general been far more productive than destructive (although this must be stated with great care in the case of certain religions, as it has resulted in incalculable bloodshed and continues to do so. But broadly speaking this is because religion has been co-opted by political divides and their militaristic advocates whose determination has been to take one side of the argument for their own ends.) The ability to absorb debate, to accommodate dialectics, has strengthened the relevance of the great religions, their robustness in the face of the complex muddle that is real life.

In an important way religions are there to encourage such questions to be asked and to act as a methodology through which answers can at least partially be worked towards. Buddhism, for example, propounds the positivism of enquiry; enquiry is growth. We are freed from the pain of clutching for permanence if we accept the continual process of change, if we ask the tough questions without fear of being unsettled by the lack of clear answers.

Religion is the most serious attempt made by humanity to infer from the mess in which we find ourselves the great pattern that threads through it all. It recognises that the worthwhile aspects of reality – its values, meaning and purpose – evade the crisp solutions proposed by science the same way as rainbows always allude the hiker. Instead we must settle for less easy answers; more grey; tougher demands on our intellect, on our faith. The way to find a path is to ask questions; to face our doubts, to dismiss our prejudices. Enquiry is part of the solution. It opens our minds to new opportunities.

Institutionalising the process of asking questions is something few companies have been bold enough to do. Asking the tough questions is a process that is usually subcontracted to groups of external management consultants. Externalising it makes it safe. Management can always disclaim the ideas. The bold firm usually goes no further than a rather lame annual piece of internal research on attitudes. The CEO is clearly answerable to shareholders but it is a rare situation indeed that the organisation is allowed to ask the tough questions about itself – 'are we doing things right? Why are we doing what we're doing? Have management got it wrong?'

The institutionalised asking of tough questions – about strategy, purpose, direction – is intensely productive and serves an important psychological purpose for all involved. It inspires positivism. Few companies have recognised that fact. Most have to hit a cliff edge to resort to self-enquiry. This book will hopefully go some way to changing that. We will see!

Path 7 They cloak themselves in mystery; they are not easily understood

'It is a myth not a mandate, a fable not a logic, by which people are moved.' (Irwin Edman)[8]

Religions trade in mystery – the mystery of how Christ could possibly have made water turn to wine or risen from the dead; who exactly was Lao Tzu; how Confucius could possibly have unified China in a single human lifetime. Reality is steeped in ineluctable mystery; that problem which for the human mind has no solution – like the sub-atomic world where the more we understand its formulation the stranger the world becomes. Religion turns such mystery into fable and uses these stories to engage us, to give us a clear sense that there is something here which is important but we can't fully grasp. The result is we strive to understand it and hence we have respect for it. Once something is fully understood it is conquered. It is human nature to have a lesser regard for something that has been conquered. It inspires no awe.

The fact that the great religions have preserved their mystery has been a significant driver of their enduring appeal to a world population facing the daily reality of doubt and frustration. The fables of salvation, of acts of redemption, the possibility of the miraculous – all have fed a thirst for that possibility. However cynical, we all at heart harbour the hope that our spirits will not simply be extinguished; that the souls of our deceased loved ones live on; that good acts will be rewarded. The fact that such mystery is admissible within the great religions sustains their relevance. They give us some hope when rationally such hope could be considered self-deluding.

Modern corporations are very different. They are increasingly readily understood. They can be broken down into divisions, into SBUs. Their financials are available on-line. The phenomenon of core competencies, and the corporate slimming that has followed in

---

[8]   See Edman, Irwin. *Philosopher's Quest*. Doubleday, 1957.

its wake, have helped accelerate the transparency. Most businesses are commodity-like – traded by investment funds, picked over by corporate raiders; scrutinised by analysts.

Does this matter? Yes! Mystique and perception play an enormous role in the financial markets. They play an even more important role for employees. The stronger the sense of mystique surrounding a firm, the more membership of it confers status, a sense of belonging – the more possibilities it holds. The more mystique surrounding it, the more value is likely to be attributed to it. It might just do something amazing.

The corporate equivalent of mystery is 'goodwill' – the packet of value that comes from no clear source and which is intangible. The greater the goodwill of the corporation, the less easily it will be understood, the more brain power, mystery and magic must be attributable to it. The commercial world is moving fast towards a situation where intangibles are the principal source of value added, where goodwill is the biggest piece of the real balance sheet (as opposed to the accrual-based, accounting balance sheet). Microsoft's actual goodwill (the difference between its market capitalisation and the assets on its balance sheet) is 93 per cent of its value. For Goldman Sachs it is 95 per cent. This compares to Alcoa at 25 per cent. Whereas Microsoft's PE is 60, Alcoa's is 23! That says something very clear.

Corporations have a chance to learn a serious tip from the oldest institutions on the planet – build mystique and with it comes talent, skills, differentiation and value. But such mystique has to be founded on a genuine benefit – the promise that membership of the community confers a sort of salvation; the opportunity to access resources, ideas and relationships that outsiders can only guess at; the potential to turn water into wine, individual knowledge into fortunes.

Summary

The lessons from the great religions are clear; long term success hinges on seven key attributes:

- An evolving and powerful framework of moral authority.
- A mutually supportive context focused on collective outcomes.
- A highly developed common language, idiom and identity.
- A clear and powerful sense of heritage and purpose.
- A continual flow of self-questioning.
- A positive, even aggressive, view of the future.
- An enduring mystique.

The reinspired corporation is one which understands these forces and actively masters them as part of its medium and long-term strategy. It understands that all else flows from them.

For firms accustomed to conventional corporate strategy and management consulting fare this is a big step. To a senior management group that views strategy as a game of chess, with the pawns of corporate assets, it is a real threat – an end to the elitist intellectual games.

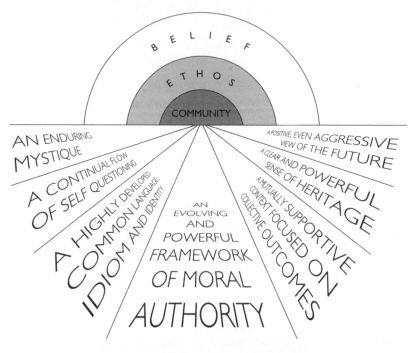

Figure 3.1 The reinspiration framework

Accordingly, the first step towards reinspiration is what could best be termed 'enlightenment' – a change in senior management mindsets. An enlightened management will recognise that medium- and long-term performance will be driven by a set of qualities not as easily determinable as the cost structure of the firm, its ROCE, ROI or EVA. While some lip service may have been paid to this in the past – a thinking-out-of-the-box session for senior management – it is unlikely that a motivational framework will have been instituted with any seriousness. The Balanced Scorecard approach may be the closest most firms have ever come.

Having accepted the road forward, having been 'enlightened', the next question is, what can be done about it? The establishment of a robust moral framework governing the collective behaviour of employees will be driven to a large extent by the firm's leadership style. The ability to cultivate a unifying language and powerful iconography will be partly driven by the firm's corporate identity policies. The willingness to promote questioning and self examination will be driven significantly by the sophistication of its internal communications process. The sense of mystique associated with a firm will be influenced by its corporate communications strategy. The creation of a mutually supportive context will be conditioned by the sensitivity of its reward and promotion system.

The key tools at the disposal of an organisation seeking to reinspire itself are not the usual 'hard' tools associated with structural change or process reengineering. They are not geared to asset allocation, financial or efficiency measurement, the redeployment of resource, the restructuring of process flows or the realignment of competencies. If there is one common thread to them, it is various forms of communications – the soft skills that do not usually sit comfortably with consultants or strategists. They are skills that are likely to be underdeveloped in most corporations. They have probably been regarded as somewhat peripheral. Putting them to work requires co-ordination between unlikely bed-fellows within the organisation such as marketing, HR and IT.

The rest of this book focuses on the very practical issue of how a firm can achieve reinspiration and what skills it needs to develop to do so. In many firms the reason these skills are underdeveloped is that their role, their contribution to the competitiveness of the firm have never been clearly defined or understood. They have no clear purpose. Managerially they have had no real home. The process of reinspiration should hopefully change all that.

Importantly, the reinspiration process is not mutually incompatible with the other developmental processes occurring within a firm. All firms periodically need to take out costs to respond to fluctuations in demand. All firms will from time to time need to re-examine the composition of their portfolios – targeted, high fit acquisitions are a necessity at a time of global consolidation. But these are periodic adjustments. Reinspiration is different. It is continuous. Once begun it will initiate a continual wave of self-renewal.

But before we go further down that road we must answer the most important question of all – what is in it for the average employee?

4

Corporate reinspiration: what's in it for the individual?

The role of work: the personal path to reinspiration

We have only talked about reinspiration from the perspective of the company, its shareholders and management. This is, of course, by definition less than half the equation. Unless a strategy works for individual managers and employees it does not work at all in the long run. Full stop.

We live in an extraordinary age where our place of work plays an unprecedented role in our lives. Most of us spend half our breathing hours working, probably more time than we spend with our families or indeed, reflecting on our own. The average knowledge worker puts in a 55-hour week versus a white-collar worker in the 1960s clocking up an average of 39 hours. The company in a real sense is the dominant institution in our lives and our progress through this institution is called our career – literally where we have come from and where we are going. The span of our achievements, our contribution, what gives our existence meaning, is measured on the yardstick of the career ladder.

This has not always been so. Until about 30 years ago, the majority of us had other institutions in our lives. Probably the thing which has changed most is our religious life, or at least its social manifestation – participation in the society of the Church. In 1900 the average Anglo-Saxon spent 4 hours per week in some sort of church-related activity. Today it stands at 0.5 hours. The absolute time spent in devout genuflection isn't the point. Closely bundled with the ritual of churchgoing were other social institutions such as community and the extended family. Along with the decrease in worship, and for closely related reasons of increased mobility and self-determinism (which has on the whole been a good thing), these institutions have also fallen into relative decline in the West. It is rare that we know more than 20 per cent of the inhabitants of our neighbourhood. It is rarer still that more than 20 per cent of our extended family live in the same city.

Most of this change has absolutely been for the better. Rigid social hierarchy has broken down – a smart person can earn more than most indolent trust-funders ever could. Women are, to a significant degree at least, integrated into the knowledge workforce. But it has come at a price. Such institutions served an important psychological role in all our lives. They provided order, a framework, a sense of structure. We all need order. We all need a sense of purpose. That need has not gone away.

So what has replaced these institutions in fulfilling these needs? Potentially, at least, the company or, in the case of the 23 per cent of us who work in companies of more than 1000 employees, the Corporation. In a sense we have come full circle. A hundred years ago the Quaker-type firms, such as the Cadburys and Kelloggs of the world, supported entire communities from cradle to grave. They were intertwined with the fabric of local communities, paying for housing and amenities. While this paternalistic policy persists to a degree in rare cases, most large firms are no longer rooted to single communities. They are global. Their manufacturing bases are dispersed and ever shifting. They are a community without geography, comprised of a network that continually changes location. They are communities (or potentially so) but of a very different nature to the geographical manufacturing communities of their antecedents.

It is also worth noting that the larger global corporations are also probably more powerful than the average nation-state and the global communities of such firms often feel more allegiance to each other than to the country in which they happen to live. The firm will be the driver of their career and prosperity, not directly their government. To the knowledge worker the nation-state is an institution of rapidly declining relevance.

What, then, does this mean for the corporation? It means its role in society is more structural than ever before. It also means it has both a responsibility and an opportunity. The responsibility is that it should, in principle, endeavour to give those employees whose waking lives are largely devoted to it, the sense of meaning, fulfilment and purpose that other institutions were once there to provide. The opportunity is that, should they provide the right degree of fulfilment and purpose, they have a unique opportunity to monopolise and harness the passions of their employees.

Of course, this begs the question, is the average firm up to it? Moral passion only comes from having a grand purpose that is spiritually fulfilling, a purpose beyond simply a pay package, beyond a time-serving sense of duty. The answer in the case of most firms is certainly no! Ask the average educated, mobile employee how driven they feel about serving their firm and what do you hear? It tends to be salutary. 'Sure. It's great learning opportunity. How committed am I? Well, how committed are they . . . ?'

The evidence suggests not very. The average tenure of the Fortune 500 CEO has fallen from ten years in 1970 to around four years in 1997. The average length of employment of the educated middle manager running an SBU has done the same thing. Ask the same manager how well he or she understands the firm's strategy; how strongly they identify with the firm's culture; how readily they can articulate the corporate mission. If you're posing the questions in the bar after hours then the honest answers you receive will be troubling. The relationship between the firm and the skilled manager or employee has never been more conditional and cynical.

Despite continual avowals to the contrary, most firms have continued to overlook the single most important driver of their long-term growth – the emotional commitment of their collective talent to the long-term success of the company; that they share the ethos of the firm; that they share a corporate sense of mission which is bigger than the edict of the CEO, which is bigger than the size of the bonus pool. This book argues that most larger firms are missing a fabulous opportunity. Returning to where we began this chapter, the company is the most important community, the primary formal structure in the majority of educated people's lives. It provides meaning; it provides purpose. The need is there. The opportunity is there. All the firm needs to do is learn to respond to it.

The modern HR box of tricks

The modern corporation is not, of course, entirely blind to what we are talking about. The growth in popularity of stock options, long-term incentive plans that pay out over a number of years and the shift to engaging employees as pseudo shareholders, are all expressions of the recognition that, unless a bond of mutuality is re-established, then the company is unacceptably vulnerable.

Linking the psychological benefits of being a shareholder with the status of being an employee does work. The best examples are probably to be found among the professional services businesses which are still structured as partnerships. The one-firm ethic of businesses such as Arthur Andersen or McKinseys has allowed these firms to expand at tremendous rates while maintaining the integrity of their culture and identity globally. Andersen Consulting alone has grown from 25 000 professionals in 1990 to around 65 000 today. The shareholders are all in the business and therefore their bond to the firm and with each other is inviolable. As a result, these well-educated professionals tend to invest an unusual amount of both their time and their emotional energies in these firms. They are in a real sense 'McKinseyites' or, in that rather unfortunate acronym, 'Androids'. We will examine professional service firm structures in more detail in the following chapters. The model is a useful one.

Industrial firms have been quick to follow suit. The evolving terminology such firms tend to use is telling, most significantly the concept of 'stakeholders'. Stakeholdership as a concept is meant to denote unification of the interests of shareholders and employees in a sort of communal utopia. Its principal tool is the stock option. In some firms, notably the higher growth newcomers such as Microsoft, options plans are indeed distributed deep in the organisation – to the point that the overhang of unexercised options is monstrous. But in most firms serious options plans are limited to the top dogs. The real stakeholders are the bosses. *Plus ça change* . . .

The options approach is also of dubious sustainability. It can super-ficially appear fine in periods of high industry revenue growth and general share price appreciation. The faster employees push the revenue line, the further the stock will rise. But this does not hold in periods of slowdown or intense competition based on price. In this situation the immediate interests of shareholders may be best served by cutting headcount, paring back costs and focusing on margins rather than the top line. Suddenly, the umbilical cord linking share-holders to employees is a barrier rather than an aid. And one thing you can bet – it will be cut swiftly.

More fundamentally, we have to question whether the linkage of remuneration structures and shareholder value actually contributes to driving the long-term competitiveness of the firm. Does 'excess' bonus money above and beyond competitive base pay really motivate people in the right way? Let's take the most extreme example – investment banking. Most of the Bulge Bracket Investment Banks are now quoted. The average banker will receive a bonus in excess of 50 per cent of his or her basic salary, paid annually following the close of the year end. In a very real sense the earnings per share of the business and hence the stockprice (as measured by the net present value of cash flows per share) and the earnings of employees are intimately related. In most other businesses the average bonus as a percentage of base salary will hover around the 5 per cent mark, max.

So does this mean the I Banks make great stocks for shareholders to invest in? Do they produce reliable, consistent, long-term returns for shareholders? The answer interestingly is no. I Banking stocks are notoriously volatile – almost as volatile as the churn rate of their employee base. Large annual bonuses linked to earnings performance have interestingly promoted a culture of intense short termism. The average professional stays in his or her firm for only three years. Psychologically a banker is first a banker and then an employee of a specific firm. Has this damaged individual banks in the medium term? Probably. Differentiation between Investment Banks is ever tougher to determine, a great deal of business is shifting to a cost basis and it can be anticipated that average margins will not increase. Most Investment Banks have made up the shortfall with proprietary trading – and thereby increased the volatility of their earnings. Fortunately for the investment banking community, the development of the global capital markets is careering ahead at a tremendous pace, driving product innovation and sustaining margins.

What is the way out of the box?

So, given the fact that employee churn does appear to be increasing, can firms realistically hope to reverse it by strengthening the mutual bond between firm and employee? Or are employees and employers now divorced beyond redemption?

Interestingly, while the bond between person and company has been stretched to breaking point, as we have observed, the relevance of such a bond to the individual has probably never been greater. Individuals only derive a sense of purpose, meaning and fulfilment in the context of interacting with other people. We are all essentially social beings and the social role of company life is central to most of our lives.

We should point out that this runs counter to much of contemporary management thought. The driving logic of most contemporary thinking is towards the individualisation of work, the de-corporatisation of careers. Freelancers working alone in their spare bedrooms perform analytical and research functions for corporations which previously would have been handled by employees. Employees themselves shift from having full-time status to being consultants. The firm loses a fixed cost and the employee often, ironically, earns more.

Even inside companies the dominant swing is towards fragmentation. P&L management has mostly been pushed down to the lowest unit of operation. Managers of SBUs are encouraged to expand their businesses entrepreneurially. The concept of intrapraneurialism is there to satisfy the manager's desire for autonomy and creativity while yielding the benefits and upside to the firm. While in principle, managerial 'empowerment' is clearly healthy (with the limitations that term implies), it is also too often used as an excuse to squeeze immediate profit out of every asset in the company by measuring performance on the most desegregated basis possible. Decentralisation is often merely a euphemism for cost elimination.

The evolution of IT networks has clearly propelled the ability of organisations to eliminate old bureaucratic structures and free up the individual to operate more autonomously. This is clearly an intensely positive process. Giving people degrees of latitude to experiment, to express their creativity, to innovate, is a profoundly energising process for a company. But it is no good unless it happens within a supportive framework which guards collective purpose and provides broader meaning. It is easy for firms to do away with everything that does not drive revenue, until all that exists in an organisation are people operating on commission or day rates. The virtual company is also an empty company.

Counter to this logic of fragmentation, the social need for belonging is there in the majority of people. Computer links don't inspire people; e-mail doesn't constitute social connectedness –

contrary to the hype. Most people want to feel they are part of a community of like-minded individuals. They want to believe in the collective group with whom they work. They want affirmation, acknowledgement and confederacy. Most people want to know that at the foundation of their lives there is something solid, something admired which they can feel good about having contributed to and which, in turn, they know will be there for them when they need support. As Jack Welch once observed, 'the most important thing we have is our sense of belonging and contributing to something great.' We all have a need for endorsement. This endorsement gives us purpose. It gives our lives meaning. Through it we gain a sense of our own identity, an identity which is socially and not individually defined.

Interestingly, this 'community role' is one which (with the exception of the handful of avuncular Quaker businesses we have already mentioned) the company would not historically have had a principal claim to fill. Probably the dominant legitimate institutional claimant to occupying this role has been the Church – the organisation that for centuries has been the ultimate provider of institutional meaning. The Church still plays a significant role in the social structure of a large proportion of people's lives. Aside from any spiritual solace, its social function is pivotal to many communities, from India to Indiana. The ritual of weekly gathering, the pastoral role of the priest, the contribution of funds. All of these rituals embed meaning in people's lives and provide a backbone of social order. The 'Church', although an international institution in terms of shared religious doctrine, is fundamentally local in its manifestation to most people – a priest, a place and local custom. The combination of local, adaptive meaning against a backdrop of universal doctrine is its most powerful dialectic – giving a grand concept a local meaning and a name.

The decline of the institutions of the West has been contiguous with the growth of the nuclear family – the movement away from community and larger social affiliations. The corporation has a wonderful chance to assume the mantel of this role and in so doing transform the basis of its competitive advantage.

Of course, that sounds all very well and good. But in practice how can a firm do so? What are the practical steps? How sure can it be that this is the road to competitive advantage? What will the impact be on EPS? That is the road we will continue down in the remaining chapters of this book.

Summary

The acid test of any future management concept or approach is that it serves the emotional needs of the assets that drive the value of a business – and those assets are people. It is hopefully clear that there is a yawning need for meaning, for fulfilment and for social endorsement among most employees, a need that can only probably be met in the workplace. Those businesses that endeavour to meet this need will thrive. Those that fail to do so will flounder in mediocrity. When we, as old people, have the privilege of looking back, that will be the great distinction between the winners and losers of the next few decades.

5

Path 1: Reinstating a framework of moral authority

The decline of corporate strategy

For the last 20 years senior managers and consultants have focused their efforts on the fine art of corporate strategy. If any CEO was asked what their principal responsibility is in the battle to maximise shareholder returns it would be forging a coherent strategy. The notion of corporate strategy as the driving principle behind good management is fundamentally embedded in contemporary thinking. Not 30 seconds goes by in the average MBA classroom without the term being wheeled out.

The concept of corporate strategy is not in fact an old one. It was thrust into the limelight with the explosive growth of the management consultants – Bain, BCG, McKinsey, Booz Allen – in the 1970s and then enshrined as an executive religion by Michael Porter's books *Competitive Strategy* (1980) and *Competitive Advantage* (1985). It had taken a full 150 years for the terminology Clauswitz applied to the battlefield to get formally translated to the managed conflict that is modern business.[1]

---

[1] See Clausewitz, Carl Von. *On War*. Penguin, 1983.

At heart, the concept of corporate strategy says that a firm is there to be steered, to be restructured, to be redirected by the organisation's leaders. Corporate strategy requires a clear, dirigistic path to be laid out – which markets, which products, what pricing, etc. And strategy, the logic follows, is only as good as the thinking at the top. It takes the view that the kingdom without a king is nothing. Not surprisingly, therefore, the ascendancy of corporate strategy has been contiguous with the birth of the star CEO and, following close on their heels, the management consultants to advise them. The fact that writings concerned with feudal wars between petty monarchs, such as Clausewitz's *On War* or Sawyer's *The Art of the Warrior*,[2] have translated so happily into corporate strategy clearly says something about the way management is viewed by the strategists. Firms, like armies, are there to be marshalled and ordered unquestioningly into battle.

For a period of 20 years, the unabating conviction has remained that what determines a corporation's success is the quality of its strategy and how effectively the top management team implement it. This conviction has driven the phenomenal shuffling of the corporate decks we have already discussed. Major firms have been merged, divested, reengineered, acquired, principally on the basis of one corporate strategy or another, even if, as is so often the case, it was post-rationalised. While corporate strategy has, on the whole, cleaned out the worst of the corporate sloppiness of the 1970s and early 1980s, it inevitably succumbs to the short-term tactics we enumerated in Chapter 2. It is the chess game.

Things are beginning to change. The average corporation is now an intensely complex beast, principally as a result of internationalisation. Twenty years ago your average company might have had 70 per cent of its sales in its home market and what it exported it manufactured at home. That ratio now looks almost inverted. The result is an organism with many moving parts, many of which both in style and approach might be quite alien to management back home. In

---

[2]   See Sawyer, Ralph D. *The Art of the Warrior: Leadership and Strategy from the Chinese Classics.* Shambhala Publications, 1996.

this new context traditional corporate strategy is fundamentally clumsy. Using a Big Bertha driver doesn't work well when negotiating sand traps on an unfamiliar Scottish Links. The top manager has, albeit reluctantly, to accept that many decisions which he might consider strategic have to be taken close to the local market or within the individual business unit. Imposing corporate strategy conceived several thousand miles away on the strong managers needed to sustain an international organisation does not work.

Formal corporate strategy does not respond flexibly to this new complex reality. Nor can it accommodate the organic development process that underlies most organisations. There are only so many times the decks can be artificially reshuffled. Eventually you actually have to let the organism of the firm flourish and demonstrate organic growth. The interesting thing is that were the Boards of most large firms to actually stop strategising, they would discover that the rate of organic growth of the firm would probably not slow. It might actually pick up! Wonder of wonders! The organisation would appear to have a life of its own, even in the absence of a corporate strategy. They would find smart managers adapting core knowledge to local, particular needs and winning. They would find feedback seeping back to the centre and conditioning corporate decision-making. That phenomenon is called organisational learning. It is an organic process stimulated by the organisational imperative to grow and replicate. It has little to do directly with strategy.

This observation is (hopefully!) profoundly unsettling for many top managers used to instituting corporate strategy like a surgeon sewing on a fresh limb, backed up by the friendly consulting firm from London, New York or Boston. What it says is that perhaps corporate strategy is not what matters. What matters is that the organisation has an ability to ensure all these dispersed, individual efforts are constructive rather than destructive, that its organic process is in balance and likely to produce a bigger, more stable entity. Having a thousand managers scattered round the globe building their micro businesses could lead to a nightmare of Balkanisation. They have to be pulling to the same tune.

So what is the glue, the DNA ensuring the molecules adhere into a whole? It cannot be corporate strategy which only has an average 3-year life-span. It cannot be a management consultant's report. This is where the 'moral framework' comes in. A moral framework ensures that individual efforts occur within a context of shared objectives, shared methods and shared 'ideology'.[3] It is a code of self-governance. It is the framework on which the web of human processes and relationships that make up a company hang. It lends them a coherence and makes the collective actions of the company unique in their order.

The strategic plans of most large businesses focus obsessively on outputs – EPS, ROS and sales growth. Inevitably, the more stringent they become, the more the firm will tend to focus on costs as these are what can be most actively predetermined. Revenue forecasting is tough and since strategic targets must be met, costs become the inevitable centre of attention. Corporate strategy focuses on assets.

The reinspired corporation has a very different conception of purpose in which, like any organism, it seeks to extend and propagate itself. The firm's moral framework shapes those characteristics it legitimately aims to propagate – what the community of the firm believes in and those qualities that constitute its essential character and condition the manner in which it seeks to export its beliefs.

Whereas corporate strategy is usually represented as a series of analytical boxes, a moral framework is a lattice that supports the community of the company. This lattice defines how the firm tackles the challenge of doing what it does – the delivery of value. It defines how the organisation makes what it delivers to customers unique from any other firm – *'the way things are done here'*. This lattice is reinforced by the other six elements of reinspiration – by the strength of its shared identity, the relevance of its heritage, the tolerance for idea exchange and dialogue, the intensity of shared aspiration and

---

[3] 'Ideology' means the root of an idea shaping how a community governs itself. The idea has unfortunately been appropriated as a political term of disapprobation, particularly by the political right.

the perceived value of membership of the community. This lattice governs the way relationships are managed both inside and outside the firm – 'this is how we behave . . .'.

But what a moral framework is not is a behavioural rule book. 'Thou shalt not . . .' is an anachronistic coda strait-jacketing people into a formalistic way of behaviour. Such precepts have been consigned to the scrap heap along with the old command and control led structures. Moral authority as a rule book is meaningless. It does not compel. It does not provide meaning. It is not a model of behaviour that anyone can believe in any more than the average line manager believes in corporate strategy.

So the dominant characteristic of the moral framework of the firm is that it is motivational, not regulatory. (In this respect it differs from the Balanced Scorecard.) To act as a motivating but guiding force, it has to be morally defensible – to incline people to do what is right. It also has to be conducive to self-improvement and betterment, otherwise it will not enthuse. Finally, it cannot be personalised uniquely in the figure of the CEO or it will no longer be a framework of self governance but a top management dictate. These three characteristics underpin a potent moral framework – demanding that such a framework constitutes:

1   A solid moral foundation.
2   A methodology for self-betterment.
3   An impartial law of self-governance.

Let's examine each of these qualities in turn.

A framework, sure. But why moral?

Why do we call it a 'moral' framework? Morality smacks of stultification, of old-school self-righteousness. But to feel good about what one does, one at some level has to feel it is right; that it constitutes the fulfilment of good, respectable intentions. Acting morally commands respect in a community which is healthy and robust. Acting 'morally' is essentially an endorsement of one's legitimate claim to participation in a community. No individual operates according to a personal moral code (now that the Wild West is long gone!). We do not define what is right and wrong alone unless we are self-deluding or a tyrant! Morality is defined by the social group we are linked to. It underpins any society, delineating between good and bad.

In the religious world morality has a strict set of meanings most clearly enunciated as 'commandments'. The communities of the corporate world are very different in this respect. The definition of what is right, what is laudable is not fixed or absolute. It is not governed by anything as universalistic as the Ten Commandments or Five Pillars. For one group of people being the most cost competitive producer of goods or services for customers can constitute the moral high ground. For another, being the most innovative in meeting market needs will command respect. Beyond such generic categories, the community of the company will have its peculiar sense of what constitutes the moral high-ground, what they as an organisation seek to propagate, what they seek to be respected for.

Firms that are highly differentiated as communities tend to have a clear sense of what they stand for, which in turn conditions the nature of the product or service they deliver. Their sense of fulfilment stems from a strong conviction that their approach to satisfying customers is morally laudable. They feel good about what they do. Work is a personal and collective moral fulfilment. They have a missionary zeal to enlighten as many people and markets as they possibly can.

Morals versus values

The management literature is increasingly full of this elusive, chimerical term 'values'. Firms are exhorted to identify their core values, enshrine them in lists and emblazon them daily on screensavers. The feeling at the back of even the most receptive senior manager's mind must be one of cynicism.

The term 'values' is a hopeless simplification of a highly complex reality. Identifying values is an entirely inadequate way to describe the complexity of a moral framework. A moral framework that works is active, conditioning and inescapable. It defines our aspirations; it prescribes what makes us admired by our peers; it isolates those things we strive to achieve. It works through us. The values to which it gives rise may be listed out. But that is the same as describing the colours of the sea. The sea evolves continually and it has many other dimensions in addition to colour.

Moral frameworks are not delicate protocols enshrined in gold-leafed books. They tend to be highly competitive, highly self-selecting. They continually test us. As we as a community change, so the framework shifts with us. This is where the religions are unparalleled. They do not promulgate values. The 'commandments' are only one aspect of them. They provide a robust, although ambiguous, framework encompassing all aspects of our lives, through which we can manage our relationship with ourselves and with other people.

The concept of 'values' is comfortable to managers because they are susceptible to the orderliness of strategy. For the same reason they are intensely limiting. It is tempting for a Board to declare that the organisation will uniformly devote itself to good customer service, on-time delivery, innovation, etc. This may have a satisfying ring of tidiness but it does not take the community of the firm forward. It is hollow and incredible.

The concept of values is also easily hi-jacked by communities whose moral framework is fundamentally defunct. Any group can use a claim of well-enunciated values to justify an indefensible position. The number of examples littering history are too vast to enumerate. A moral framework is far more difficult to falsify because its constituent parts are more subtle, demanding and above all because it is nothing unless lived out by its subscribers and adherents. It cannot be identified in the form of a list.

The power of attaining the moral high ground, of doing what is morally laudable is tremendous. Firms that can do so with justification are almost invariably winners. The continuing ascendancy of the diminutive Virgin Airlines over British Airways is one example of many. The continued growth of Johnson and Johnson in the wake of its principled across-the-board withdrawal of Tylenol, following contamination of the product, is another. Once a firm is set on such a cause, a cause for the right of the customer and employee, then it gathers its own momentum. The moral objective is the one that fundamentally matters to people.

The imperative to self-betterment

To be effective, a moral code cannot simply be a method of governance – it cannot be the same as a list of values or a mission statement. As with the great religions, is also has to be a framework for personal redemption. It is something that guides behaviour through managing aspirations. Unless it holds the prospect of self-betterment, both moral and material, then it can never stimulate.

Most self-respecting people strive for self-betterment, both in terms of skills and social acknowledgement. We all want to be endorsed as winners by our peer group. As we discussed in Chapter 3, a moral code is a framework through which people can work towards such fulfilment. Such a framework underpins any community, binding it together with a shared regard for what constitutes success. It comes with guidelines for achieving such success, and anecdotes about those that have succeeded before.

It is fundamentally different from corporate strategy in this regard. Corporate strategy imposes a view on an organisation which it has to adopt. It drives discrete episodes of change. A moral framework, with its route to self-advancement, is something that is learnt, which infuses one's personal development, that evolves over time. One learns to succeed by mastering those qualities the community holds in high esteem. As such, it is fundamentally more motivating because it is elicited, not imposed.

Most management teams recognise that to get people to do things there has to be personal gain and a clear relationship between cause and effect. Consequently, the usual focus tends in most instances to be on that crudest form of incentive – cash. As we have already discussed, the investment banking industry has taken this equation to an extreme. But it has not created stable firms producing high returns for shareholders. Cash as a motivator is vastly over-rated (and vastly expensive!). A moral framework, by contrast, motivates by driving a process of education, of acquisition of skills that will better the employee's ability to contribute to the community and thereby win social endorsement. The end is moral because it is the fulfilment of a valued societal role, not the filling of a personal cheque account.

Leadership and the moral framework

The biggest error most firms commit is mistaking strong leadership for a strong moral framework. A moral framework is by its very nature impersonal and organic. But, of course, that is a very unfashionable proposition in a time of intense individualism.

Leadership is a highly polarised concept in modern corporate life. It is literally interpreted as connoting the charisma and competence of an individual. The last 50 years have also seen the ascendancy of the creed of the individual in everyday life. If you turn to the papers the focus is on the profile and achievements of individuals, if you switch on the TV the dominant preoccupation is with celebrities. The concept of celebrity is metamorphosed into a cult in publications such as *Hello!*. The medium of TV in particular has thrust the individual into the spotlight – both film stars and politicians.

Was this ever any different? Is humankind any less gripped by the love lives of the Spice Girls than they were by the peccadilloes of Byron? The individualisation of society is, of course, not simply a product of the explosion of media, although that has undoubtedly accelerated the process. It is more fundamentally driven by the decline of institutions. We have already touched on the well-documented demise of the community social structure. In a period where the mobility of labour will increase and not decrease this process will, if anything, simply accelerate. Shared values, common moral standards – all these unifying precepts – have been swallowed up by the ascendancy of individual determination and expression.

What does this mean for the world of business? Well, things are no different here. The world of business, like society at large, has been individualised. The role of the CEO is probably the most glaring example. Some useful facts here: the average CEO running a firm of more than 10 000 employees has an average tenure in the job of four years, down from eight years in 1970. The average fixed and variable compensation of that CEO, measured in terms of cash and stock options, is fifty times that of the average employee in the firm. In some well-documented instances this multiple shoots into three digits.

The question we must ask is, what does this say about the imputed role of the CEO? First, the modern CEO is attributed by institutional shareholders (who will typically nowadays have a key say in the appointment of a CEO) as having the capability to produce material changes in the performance of even major corporations, and to do so within a short space of time. The role of the CEO will be analogous to that of the coach of a football team that has lost six games in a row – to get them back on track fast and boost EPS. This view has two critical facets: it is short-term results oriented; and the CEO is cast as the star – the man or woman with the strategy.

Is this realistic? Is it viable in the long term? First, a fact: a football team has up to 30 players performing a set of discrete, co-ordinated tasks in a finite period of time. A corporation is a mass of complex activities, performed by a vast network of skilled people, each project and undertaking with very different time scales. The football team is recomposed each season. While it will have a collective history, its actual continuity is low. A major corporation (leaving aside the first generation businesses such as Microsoft, Dell, etc.) will have evolved over decades; it has customs, values, ways of doing business which tend to be communicated from one generation to the next. In such a situation, when dealing with an organism more than a team, is it reasonable to believe the coach solution will work? Will it produce a more competitive company in the long run?

Institutional investors would almost invariably answer yes. This belief is founded on what the average star CEO has been doing over the past decade. This brings us back to the dreaded term reengineering. In a decade of efficiency measures and cost reduction, the ability of the CEO to deliver significant EPS enhancement over a discrete period of time has been high. Taking out costs tends to produce an immediate earnings benefit. The legendary Chainsaw Al of Sunbeam fame delivered what institutions wanted (although not at Sunbeam as it happened!). The KKR-style break-up and re-capitalisation have produced handsome returns. The claim that a single individual can make or break an organisation in a two- to three-year period has been endorsed. The only problem, of course, is that these gains are one-off. They cannot be repeated each year without the organisation being bled anaemic. The only way to create earnings growth in the medium term is revenue growth and innovation. That is a collective, organic process, not a one-man forced march.

The real issue is whether star status management will lead to high returns over the medium term. In the case of some of the high growth stocks of the last decade – Microsoft, AOL, Dell, Amazon – the founder still drives the company. In an important way the firms' ethos is still highly identified with the individual that created them in the first place – a bit like disciples receiving from a prophet, although the analogy is unfortunate! As they mature, the issue will be whether such firms can find a way to institutionalise those beliefs and moral frameworks so as to ensure organic growth.

The new conglomerates can also be misleading as examples to emulate. Over the last 20 years, as in the 20 years before that, a large number of groups have appeared from nowhere through acquisition. In the marketing communications area, for example, the three giants, Interpublic, Omnicom and WPP are all short-term creations. They are all driven by the individuals who pulled them together through force of personality as demon deal-doers. Again the cult of the individual appears to be vindicated. Shareholder value creation has been significant. However, sustainability will be a real issue once that personality glue is gone. Where the CEO is the focus of attention, the firm has by definition more than even odds of evaporating.

The firm with a strong moral framework will be more enduring than the firm reliant on an individual. (If, at one extreme, the CEO and CFO went down in a plane crash, how would this affect the average corporation's stock price?) That is not to say that a reinspired firm will not have charismatic leadership, but that the organisation will have its own momentum. In such an organisation the CEO is likely to be focused on what we have called ideology – how things are done here – not on strategy in its traditional sense. As such, they will magnify and direct the latent energy of the community of the firm.

In the reinspired corporation the CEO tends to be focused on re-energising the existing strengths of the company; the qualities that make it unique in its ability to inspire its employees to deliver exceptional services or products; which make it unique in its ability to serve both its customers' emotional and material needs. The leader will be a figure dedicated to renewal but with a vision based on key strands of continuity. Their focus will be on achieving praise for the company, not for themselves. Their own success will always be couched in terms of the company's success as a collective of individual capabilities. Instead of a single star, the firm will have a constellation of stars throughout the organisation, each of whom will serve as role-models for aspiring employees. As Lao Tzu put it more eloquently, 'A leader is best when people barely know that he exists. Of a good leader who talks little, when his work is done, his aim fulfilled, they will say "we did this ourselves"'.[4] What we have described is, of course, an anomaly.

---

[5]   See Waley, Arthur. *The Way and Its Power*. Allen and Unwin, 1958.

Towards a moral framework of management

This all sounds pretty good but is a moral framework really a viable substitute (or perhaps better termed, complement) for a corporate strategy? The answer is yes! The strength of a firm's moral framework correlates closely to its competitiveness. The more tightly knit and well articulated, the more powerful it is. The moral framework of a firm shapes the way insiders think, what they aspire to. An organisation is nothing other than a bundle of relationships. If the people creating those relationships develop along a cohesive path, the organisation will evolve accordingly. Corporate strategy may redirect its energies temporarily or shift their course, but soon enough the framework will take back over. The analogy of the river is an apt one. The flow can be blocked but the water will find a way to flow down another stream bed (e.g through the vehicle of another firm!).

It is this author's contention that the moral framework will replace the worn-out reliance on corporate strategy. Moral frameworks are the only workable forms of management in the modern corporation. In most large companies the calibre of employees is high. They will tend to know more about the particular situation of the company in specific markets than their bosses. In such circumstances, continual interventionist management from the top is dysfunctional. The only means management has for directing the company is to nourish a moral framework. Firms with strong moral frameworks, with a shared sense of what is right for employee and customer, will do better than firms that continually focus on artificially shifting the course of their flow. The management challenge is to let the flow do its work by adding to, not micro-managing its momentum.

Assuming they buy into the goal of reinspiration, the difficulty for most firms is how they can actively influence the development of the moral framework of their firm. As we have explored, a strong moral framework has three fundamental characteristics – a well-defined moral foundation, an explicit pathway to self-betterment, and

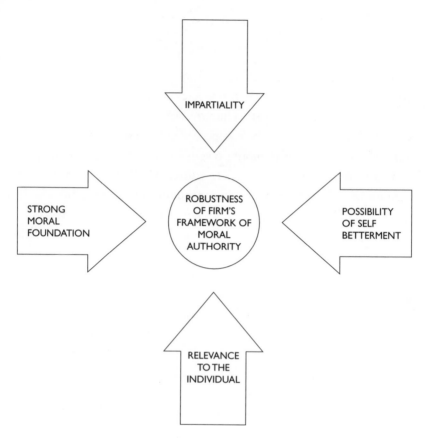

Figure 5.1 The core characteristics of a moral framework

freedom from individual management distortions or, better phrased, impartiality. Overall it also has to have a principal focus on and relevance to the individual. Its architects must acknowledge that unless the framework offers benefits that are meaningful to the individual, it will be irrelevant to the larger community. It responds to the questions of what the organisation wants to become, what the corporation is trying to deliver, what it is striving for, what it wants to achieve for itself and, most importantly, what's in it for me, the little guy? It binds the community of the firm together by defining what its members believe is their ultimate purpose and what behaviour is required of them to get there.

So, provided the core qualities of such a framework are understood, how does an uninspired organisation create the necessary conditions for evolving a strong moral framework? For a strong moral framework is not an isolated construct – it is not a list of values. It is founded on the other six elements of reinspiration. Understanding the intimate interdependence of these seven forces requires treading down the six remaining paths of reinspiration.

6

Path 2: Refocusing the corporation on collective outcomes

The rediscovery of collective purpose

Trying to get large numbers of individuals to act to achieve a common goal is the oldest challenge facing any society, whether it be a country or a company. Two people together can, on the whole, achieve far more than two people acting independently. We all know that. But it requires a compromise of the brute impulse towards the pursuit of individual goals. And that impulse is strong indeed! All of us are caught in our own prisoner's dilemma.

In order to be overcome, it requires a countervailing force equally as powerful. The question is what is that force? What drove hundreds of men to haul forty 25-ton Sarsen stones from all over England's West country into what we now know as Stonehenge – Europe's greatest prehistoric monument? If you have ever wandered amongst those monoliths at dusk, you have to marvel!

In most developing organisations, as in developing countries, the method of achieving co-operation is simple: one form or other of dictatorship, benign or otherwise. One person or a small coterie of founders conceive a purpose, a direction and around it elaborate a guiding philosophy – the way things will be done. Joiners either subscribe to it or they do not and on this basis they are either left inside or out. Should an insider raise a challenge to the guiding philosophy of the founders, then they will probably be punished with expulsion. The framework governing behaviour is proscriptive, unyielding and personalised in the figure of the leader – usually the founder. This description makes it sound a negative phenomenon which it usually is not. The excitement of early growth makes the process positive and we all respond to a strong, charismatic leader when the path is an uncertain but exhilarating one.

Social institutions, whether geopolitical units or corporations, that begin within a rigid personalised framework, will almost inevitably evolve over time to a more democratic means of self-governance. Democracy is inevitable with growth and sophistication. As a community becomes larger it is forced to decentralise management. Over time the number of significant voices grows. The complexity of development requires an adaptive strategy, a strategy that is increasingly consensus driven. It also becomes essentially depersonalised. Over time the institution begins to generate its own peculiar character, independent of any particular individual, although it might reflect in a number of ways the original founding spirit. Companies, like countries, have the same life-cycle in this respect.

The natural democratisation of management serves an essential purpose in the preservation of the competitiveness of an organisation as it grows. It is a natural adaptation among those collective structures that thrive and survive. Why? Because unless a collective body broadly reflects the interests of all participants, then it will ultimately fragment, and then dissolve. This is precisely what happens with the majority of corporations which have an average life-span of 40 years. They fail to move beyond oligarchy to a community framework that provides a compelling collective purpose to the individuals that comprise it. Pieces break away through MBOs or the resignation of key individuals. They ultimately wind up being taken over, merging or going bust.

The intense individualisation of management in mature companies (as opposed to founding partner firms) usually surfaces during

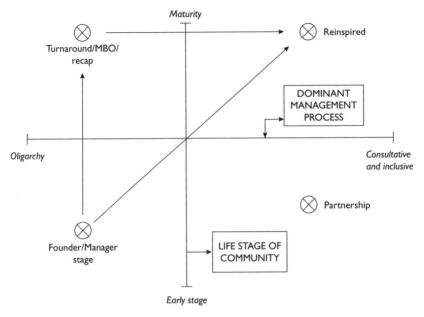

Figure 6.1 The evolution of collective purpose

intense periods of change – turnaround, recovery, or break-up – where the CEO becomes the change agent and deliberately disruptive (to the positive end of enhancing shareholder returns, of course!). This is not sustainable. The problem is that they all too often do not recognise that fact. Back to our political parallelism, political dictators similarly find it hard to give up power after a successful coup. Absolute power is intoxicating. This is the cycle of disruption many big firms find themselves in. It is indeed a very short-term fix for shareholders.

Defining collective purpose

But why after all would an individual want to share rather than take? The evidence of motivation would seem to suggest they wouldn't and this is reinforced by many modern management incentive techniques.

The answer lies in 'purpose'. Why are we doing the job we are doing? What is the ultimate driving goal?

The concept of 'purpose' is an intriguing but elusive one. What we can say for certain is that if people feel a compelling sense of collective purpose then they are capable of extraordinary self-sacrifice and extraordinary achievements. The numbers of examples scattered through history are endless, from the formation of religions to the creation of states such as Israel. Working together towards a collective goal appears to impart a joy and sense of satisfaction that solitary endeavour alone cannot deliver. In an abstract sense, the purpose of an organisation is to allow people to achieve something gratifying together.

Needless to say, most corporations and analysts see life very differently. The majority of senior managers, consultants and bankers, if asked, would subscribe to the view that the purpose of the corporation is to create shareholder wealth. They would also almost certainly say that the key to maximising the wealth-creating capacity of a corporation is the quality of leadership. The collective fulfilment of a creative need would not come into it. The majority of firms are run on the basis that their purpose is solely creation of shareholder wealth and the key to getting there is individual leadership.

The reinspired corporation, by contrast, is one where shareholder wealth is the by-product of the collective goal of becoming the best, the most admired, the most powerful institution in its sector and the means of getting there is ensuring that all employees share and are enthused by that goal. Indeed, it is a goal to which their energies naturally give rise. The role of top management in this process is ensuring that the framework to support that sense of purpose is in place. When the purpose of employees and company (meaning management) are aligned, then great things happen. But the barriers to getting there are high!

The individualisation of work

The thrust towards the individualisation of work has been inexorable over the past few years, principally, and perhaps ironically, as a result of positive forces. As firms have expanded internationally the process of local empowerment has grown with it. With the increases in the service component of most products, and the necessity for enhanced customisation of product and services, authority has inevitably been invested increasingly in the hands of the individual. The growth of network communications has also given such employees access to that critical commodity – information.

The outcome of this process of 'empowerment' has largely been positive. It has responded, even if inadvertently, to the growing awareness among most people of their responsibility to develop their personal equity. Firms have shaken off the strait-jacket of command and control, and purged themselves of their managerial bureaucracies.

However, the process also poses its problems – the fragmentation of the corporation. The advantage large organisations have over small ones is, at the risk of banality, their size. Size has great advantages. It means more ideas, more cash for ideas, better distribution, economies of scale to achieve competitive costs, greater capacity to absorb the risks associated with new products and the ability to open up new markets. Above all, size means a strong corporate personality that can stamp its mark on the hostile landscape.

The ideal, of course, is equilibrium – size combined with local agility is the golden mean to which all modern corporations must, consciously or otherwise, aspire. The danger is that once the hare of individualisation is let run, it is contagious. The balance is so easily lost. One barometer of the degree to which this balance has already been lost in many corporations is the massive explosion in management buy-outs.

To be in balance, in equilibrium, the drive to individualisation has to be offset by a benefit from collective action. This benefit cannot be solely material. It has also to be emotional. The question is, what emotionally can the individual gain from the company he or she would not get running their own one-man consultancy for 30 per cent more income?

Over the past decade most employees have smelt the coffee. They have come to view and manage their careers individually, independent of their life in a particular company. The growth of MBAs and other professional qualifications are an expression of this. The new skilled generation will focus on building their personal skill base, their résumé, their 'personal equity' and use these to gain leverage between companies towards their personal career goals. In this scenario, firms themselves become merely temporary ports of call, part of a voyage. This process of individualisation has, of course, been accelerated by the growth of outsourcing, including use of consultants as substitutes for full-time management. More structurally, the boom in IT networks is massively accelerating the rate of transfer of value from the corporate balance sheet to the personal balance sheet of skilled employees.

Corporations have collectively experienced a one-time boost in productivity over the past decade as a result of the elimination of fixed costs. However, the process of individualisation is beginning to show its side effects. Individualism is intensely corrosive to medium-term corporate success. As capital migrates from atoms to bits, most of these bits reside in the heads of people. People developing personal equity, with bits in their heads, have market power and they will use it to raise their salary and career prospects. Careers become the continual sale of one's developing intellectual assets to the highest bidder. The question is, how can the risk implicit in this process be mitigated for the firm?

The lessons of partnership structures

So how does a firm create a sense of unifying purpose? If the ancient Britons could hoist their Sarsens, some firm out there must have cracked the nut of group motivation. Perhaps the best example of collectively aligned interests are partnerships. Partnerships are liter-ally premised on all the key constituencies taking a reward based on the performance of their peer group. Partnerships are non-existent outside certain professional service areas, most notably accountancy and law. Perhaps the only exception in the industrial world is Mondragon, the Basque collective, or in the retail world John Lewis, the UK soup-to-nuts department store. The more common model in the retailing and marketing world (often focused on agricultural produce) is the co-operative. However, collectives or co-operatives are very different from partnerships. Partnerships are internally highly competitive. They behave and look to the outsider much more like normal firms.

It should be no surprise that some of the world's fastest growing companies are partnerships – McKinsey, Arthur Andersen, Price Waterhouse Coopers, to name a few. But they, in the scheme of things, are a rare breed. They are almost exclusively knowledge busi-nesses, with low capital requirements and are, by definition, reliant on smart individuals. While up until recently they have been at the periphery of the industrial world, as knowledge becomes the key industrial asset they have begun to move to centre stage. But they are still comparatively marginalised as a source of management insight.

Most firms cannot, of course, literally become partnerships. It is not feasible given the capital requirements of industrial firms and the need to have access to the capital markets. The firms which have emulated the partnership ethos within normal public market structures most closely are also intellect-intensive businesses – the software houses. Their partnership vehicle has been the stock option plan. Options are powerful tools. Their end is monetary but in the right hands they are equally about the psychological benefits of owner-ship. Microsoft has taken the stock option path to extremes. The same approach is reflected in new growth companies such as Dell, Yahoo and Amazon.com. The motivation and one-firm-firmness of these companies stand in stark contrast to many of their venerable off-line rivals.

Most industrials are most un-partnership-like in their use of options. Most options plans are restricted in meaningful percentages to the top dogs, even if that is not what the annual report claims. By contrast, in successful partnerships one often has no idea who the leader is. They will tend to be broken down into semi-autonomous business practice areas. The partnership model is, however, one which is beyond the reach of most non-professional services organisations. That leaves the issue of how to structure more meaningful group incentives.

Incentives that incentivise

So how do you get 500 autonomous people to shift the corporate equivalent of a thousand tons of Sarsen? There are a few tools in the corporate armoury of most companies, the most important amongst them often being pretty heavily oxidised with neglect or misapplication. They can be simplified into a triumvirate of three key groups:

1   structural solutions;
2   financial and promotional incentives;
3   self-betterment programmes or corporate education.

1 Structural solutions: teams versus networks

If the organisation faces a challenge to its competitiveness that requires action most CEOs and their consultants will turn first to structural solutions. Organisational structure – whether the structure of departments, business units or the corporate portfolio – is solid, clearly delineated and easily, on paper at least, movable. Therefore, the natural response to the challenge of creating one-firm-firmness has been to seek a structural solution. To be more specific, the dominant structural paradigm of the 1990s has been the 'team'.

Team concepts were born of reengineering – the structural movement to focus the organisation around process flows rather than the specialist skills-sets called departments. Reengineering acquired the idea from production cells in the manufacturing setting and it has subsequently been exported to most sectors, from advertising agencies through to the insurance industry. The irony of teams is that, while they are meant to integrate across functions, they tend to lead to organisational fragmentation. Teams work optimally with no more than 14 people. If they work well they will tend to become quite competitive with other groups, proprietorial and defensive. In essence they will start to behave like an independent firm. As a result, the larger firm risks losing the power of its wholeness.

The inadequacy of the team approach is symptomatic of the fact that the modern organisation cannot be thought of in structural terms. In reality larger companies are founded on a network of relationships, the health of which is measurable by the volume and diversity of communications. Structural solutions such as teams which cut across these networks sever the fluid medium of the network and staunch the healthy flow of information – the information that is the life-blood of any modern company. Imposing rigid structures on organic entities means either the organism dies or it finds a way to grow around the impediment – back to our tree analogy.

2 Financial incentives and promotion schemes

The universal tool used by modern corporations to condition behaviour is the compensation scheme. Money is a fundamental reason why we all work – to earn the apocryphal crust. But it is not the only reason and, indeed, not the most fundamental one. Compensation schemes tend to suffer the weakness of a logic that says that all that matters is cash. The focus on monetary incentives is intensely cynical. In essence, it says that people are motivated by survival at one extreme of the pay scale and by either greed or peer competition at the other.

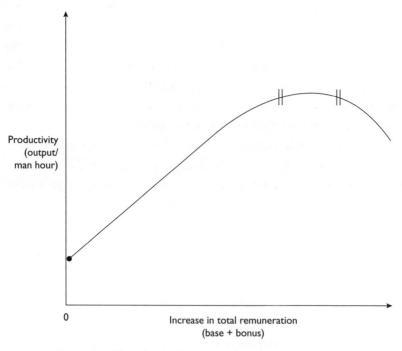

Figure 6.2 The decay function of cash as an incentive

Work of course serves a much more profound psychological purpose. Forced to retire early most people rapidly decline and, in the case of men in particular, often die prematurely. The human was meant to be employed. Once the basic requirements of mortgage payments and groceries are met, what matters is recognition and peer acknowledgement, only one crude aspect of which is met by exhibiting one's monetary stack. Consequently, financial rewards tend to have a decay function – beyond a certain point increments produce no positive effect. Bright, mature knowledge workers can also earn more after tax today by working for themselves as freelance consultants than they can in a company – typically up to 35 per cent more to be exact. This means the firm has to offer more than cash to win loyalty. The criterion has to be more sophisticated.

Heavy cash incentive schemes are also not conducive to healthy relationship networks. They focus excessively on individual performance and accentuate the emphasis on personal equity, the limitations of which we have already dealt with. Only at the periphery are they connected to notions of total firm performance, usually in the form of total shareholder returns. The assumption is that the overall performance of the company, including share price, is too remote a concept for most employees. How can they possibly affect it? Better to get them to focus on their individual tasks. This is badly misconstrued.

Most compensation schemes for mid-level and lesser employees are also intensely short-term. They tend to be linked to annual personal performance – discrete, concrete goals within the control of the individual, often enumerated as annual targets. In essence the investment span in human capital is one year only and highly conditional. It is easy in this context to understand why, once they have a positive balance in their account, talented people readily shift from employment to independent consultancy.

Perhaps the most popular means to democratise the reward process is the 360° evaluation protocol which is rapidly becoming ubiquitous. While good in its intentions, it is fundamentally weakened by being qualitative. At the end of the day, unless an individual's contribution is quantifiable, most organisations do not really take it that seriously as a driver of financial rewards. The underlying compensation methods remain the same, except there is a superficial gloss of peer review. There is nothing wrong with the intention. The error comes in the assumption that motivational tools need be linked umbilically to reward schemes and cash. Cash is not king, unless you want it to be that way.

3 Corporate education

Compensation schemes have taken massive prominence over training and development of skills which have been relatively sidelined in most businesses. They are inevitably viewed as a cost with no clear revenue stream resulting. The assumption is that cash is better spent on rewards – a sentiment driven from the top in most cases.

Training, and education are, of course, the most empowering and self-bettering investments known to man. It is the means to a better lot, of which cash is merely one by-product. It is also the means to the growth of any community. The more skilled a community, the greater its competitive advantage. Education, unlike reward schemes, is fundamentally social in nature. It is conducted in groups, it involves the transmission of knowledge from one generation to the next and tends to impart a similar way of thinking, a bond of commonality that lasts a lifetime.

Whereas the great religions tend to view education as the principal means to propagate their community, corporations have been delinquent. Most firms espouse an ethic of hiring in rather than growing one's own – usually for no better reason than to save short-term money. As a result they have been dis-intermediated. Any bright employee three years out of college will now consider an MBA course the path to self-betterment, rather than commitment to their first employer. Consequently, the equity they build up becomes their own, not their firms. They will also tend to view their career individualistically. In circumstances where knowledge-hungry firms need MBAs to replenish their ranks, the ability to cultivate a powerful, differentiated community will be very low indeed. The willingness of firms to outsource executive education to MBA institutions has probably been the biggest surrender of core value to an external supplier of the entire core-competency movement. If education is not a core competence, the firm has little chance of sustaining any unique competence at all for very long!

The way forward

The balance between the triangle of structure, incentives and education needs to shift dramatically if firms are to strengthen their communities. Few firms will find the shift an easy one. Instituting structural change initiatives is addictive – it reinforces the impression that all decisions can be taken from the top. Similarly, the

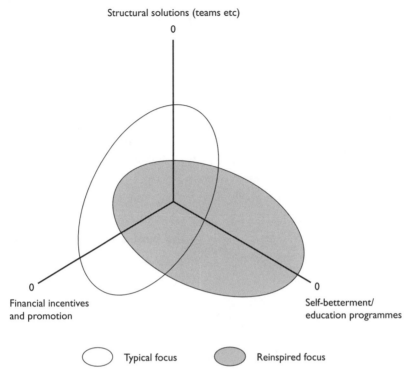

Figure 6.3 **The core drivers of community performance**

emphasis on cash reward systems is an opiate that few organisations can easily shake – the short-term incentive fix is ingrained. Education requires much more thought – a curriculum, a language, a methodology, trained educators. Most smart senior employees no longer see themselves as teachers – dissemination of knowledge would potentially undermine their personal equity. Changing that mindset requires almost Herculean efforts! The excuse often wheeled out to justify inaction is, of course, cost. If most firms dramatically reduced their use of external consultants advising them on restructuring projects and held their bonus provisions steady, more than enough cash would be created to embark on serious education programmes. It is an issue of reallocation.

It is also an issue of investment. Cash paid out as bonuses is cash burned. All it does is reward for past effort and create an obligation for payment in the future at at least the same level, if not higher – bonuses can only be reduced when there is an expectation of eliminating headcount. The same is true of cash spent on consultants who bring their knowledge to the party at a price. Cash on education, by contrast, will yield a future return. It is an investment item. Even in the shorter term there is payback. Education will pretty quickly dampen employee churn – few people leave a firm when they are learning at a steep rate – again saving budget.

Firms need turn no further than the countries in which they operate to see clearly the lesson of education. The state with the highest educated inhabitants will be the most socially cohesive and the most competitive. It's that simple! As Confucius predicted, the one with the highest wen is the winner!

7

Path 3: Cultivating a common language, idiom and identity

The importance of knowing who you are

Having a clear sense of one's own identity is as important for a company as it is for a person. Most firms understand that customers need to know what they as firms stand for. This is dealt with neatly through corporate branding and corporate advertising. This is somewhat analogous to putting on make-up and looking beautiful for strangers. What really matters is that those inside, those that care, really understand and buy into the firm's identity. As with individuals, its your friends and family that count first and foremost. The rest will follow. And they can usually see beyond the make-up! It is here that most firms fall lamentably short. They focus on looking good but do not have a good understanding of who they actually are and what they believe in. The corporate world is full of would-be catwalk models, escaping more complex psychological and sociological shortcomings! The challenge is to move from cosmetic identity to distinct corporate character based on self-understanding.

The role of symbols in shaping corporate character

To be compelling, the character of a firm must be understandable. Corporate character is most easily understood through its visual prompts that act as a route map to understanding its unique identity. The most fundamental of these visual prompts are the firm's symbols. As we have discussed, symbols play a seminal part in all our lives. They embody a set of beliefs and ideas in an immediately recognisable form, triggering clear identification of the nature of the community using them. The role of symbols is two-fold – they provide meaning and they provide a common language. They are part of the glue holding communities together.

Symbols are typically highly simplified representations. Simplification serves several purposes. First, it encapsulates an idea in a form which is universally recognisable among a group – no one is likely to fail to understand something about the significance of a crucifix. Second, it becomes easily reproducible without the loss of recognition – a cross is a cross whether it is an intricate piece of silverwork or simply two wooden sticks tied together. Hence the chance of it retaining relevance across highly dispersed geographies, where there is no documentation to explain its meaning and where it may suffer minor changes in terms of stylistic representation, is all the greater. It is a universal language within the community that gave rise to it.

Simply by seeing or feeling an icon a set of ideas are passively invoked. This invocation is closely bound up with a sense of belonging, of participation and hence is intensely social in nature. The great religions have grasped this better than any other institutions. Symbols are a language that can only be understood by a discrete group of insiders. Belonging – being in rather than out – is a fundamental driver of community. The stronger the delineation and the more highly evolved its iconography, the stronger will be the community. A community is defined by its symbols.

All the big institutions – religions, political parties and even the nation-states – have of course refined the art of symbolism as part of defining and propagating themselves. The important thing about this symbolism is that it is usually bedded in some formative event – it carries a seminal fable. The Stars and Stripes represent the formation of the federation of states, the Union Jack the melding of fractious regions. The other important characteristic of seminal symbols is longevity. These symbols are not changed for trivial reasons. They tend to last for at least several hundred years unaltered in terms of their fundamentals. This means they are not subject to passing fashion. They embody a historic truth. And this truth becomes more incontrovertible as time passes. They define the group heritage.

Corporate tattoos: the logo

Corporations, by contrast, on the whole give symbolism lip-service. The level of sophistication often stops at the cutesy corporate logo which gets changed every few years. Corporate branding programmes tend at their worst to have trivialised the power of symbols. This 'tactical' symbolism is not really symbolism at all. It is purely graphical branding. There tends not to be any root in a formative event – there is no fable, no folklore. Such identities are, on the whole, artificially engineered. When companies merge one identity is discarded and another adopted much like a corporate change of clothes. In 1998 in the US alone 240 major corporations changed their identities. This means annually a whole history of iconography gets swept away and with it all the meaning, heritage and values wrapped up with it.

There has been an increasing fascination with the power of branding among major corporations. The US spend on corporate identity branding fees shot up from roughly a billion dollars in 1980 to almost $3 billion in 1998 and is still climbing. There are many reasons for this but probably the two most important drivers have been the rate of merger and acquisition and the pace of globalisation. Both have given birth to an almost messianic mission among senior management to harmonise and render coherent otherwise diverse assets – an orderly, uniformly branded set of companies no longer looks like a portfolio and appears more like a single company. And that attracts higher ratings from the capital markets.

The usual underlying reason the clothes get changed is, of course, because the CEO wants to stamp his or her individual mark. If they want to indicate a change of strategy, a new orientation, a new regime, one of the things that usually comes in for attack first is the corporate identity. Once again, we are back to the individualisation of the firm with all the intense limitations that implies for cohesive and enduring power.

The other reason for the fascination with corporate brands is, of course, valuation. Firms have begun to ascribe value to corporate brands and put them on the balance sheet. This can enhance net asset values and hence ratios for creditworthiness. The valuation process is badly misconstrued. The key power of corporate iconography is the ability to influence the collective purpose of the company. It is a tool, not an output. It cannot be valued in the same way as a consumer brand which influences preference and premium. Many corporate identity initiatives in general still suffer from this limitation of a focus on branding – an employee does not interact with their firm the same way they do with a can of Coke!

From logo to iconography

Religious iconography is a more highly evolved form of visual symbolism than conventional corporate identity. For a start it tends to be a visual language rather than an extension of branding. Any one party to that religion will understand something by the lettering on altars, the shape of architectural features, the language of psalms. As a language it tends to be highly adaptable and to permeate all aspects of that community – there is no mistaking a Muslim lintel, text or prayer mat from the mosques of Istanbul to the Medinas of Marrakech. The values it connotes are deeply ingrained, and cannot be subjected to banal simplification. It also is organic, evolving through a continual process of reinterpretation while preserving the core historical essence. Above all, it tends to have personal relevance to all people who belong to that community. It gives a big idea a local place and name.

These same characteristics do not unfortunately typify your bog-standard branding programme. Logo schemes are rarely adaptable. They will be governed by strict guidelines, specifying the font that must be used, the precise colours, the exact configuration on a page. These programmes are policed by 'logo-cops'; they are regulated for uniformity. The driving impulse is to render the vaguely chaotic, organic nature of most firms which have evolved across different countries over time, into something that is the same everywhere. It is the Coke dream.

The reality with companies, however, is that they are not a bottle of Coke. They are organic, living cultures that rely on highly dispersed individual efforts. Binding them cosmetically behind a common image is usually a self-deluding folly of the Board wishing to assert control, wishing to package the business for easy presentation to analysts. Corporate identities driven by this impulse tend to be shallow. They mean nothing of any depth – no beliefs. Like a brand they simply foster endorsements.

As a result, such cosmetic identity programmes tend to come and go much like a fashion item. Meanwhile the heart and guts of the organisation simply move forward in its organic, somewhat autonomous fashion, like a horse that the children have dressed up as a reindeer yet again. Testimony to this is the fact that many large organisations go through a complete identity re-invention every five years, nipping and tucking their graphic physiognomy as if it were cosmetic surgery.

Perhaps the most classic example of the cost of the cosmetic brand approach to identities has been the BA make-over. British Airways recently discovered to its cost the value of iconography when it scrapped its old livery and assumed that a fancy spray-job would reboot a somewhat tired and arrogant service culture. The Union

Jacks went and were replaced by a jazzy panoply of international tail-fin art that looked good but bore no relation to the heritage of the firm whatsoever. Robert Ayling, the company's CEO, has recently rescinded his error and begun to revert to an established iconography he thought was superannuated. The damage to the value of the firm has been dramatic, as reflected in declining passenger numbers and stock price.

Imposing uniform logo systems is not the same as sharing a common language or iconography. Iconography is a graphic language that typically evolves organically over time, that accommodates reinterpretation while retaining a style, an essence that is unmistakable. Because it can be used by its community, adapted and evolved, it is a language. A language is a medium, not an object. Language is closely bound up with culture and the ethos of a community. It cannot simply be repainted.

From iconography to language

All the great religions have placed primacy on their texts more than their visual icons. The written word is powerful. It has always carried weight. What we read we tend to give credence to. The legal contractual process which underlies all our societies is one of textualisation. That is why the core of the great religions are their texts.

Many firms assume that identity is all about appearance. We live in an age where visual stimuli have assumed total ascendancy over written information. Again, it is driven by the same force of branding. Everyone understands that red and wavy lettering means a sweet syrup laced with caffeine called Coke. Visuals translate fast and are immediately and pretty universally intelligible with the back-up of global advertising. They are adaptable to mass media and mass media is the easy way to get your voice out fast. Networking takes far longer and requires patience.

The focus on visual branding cues has been strongly promulgated by the advertising groups that tend to be the landlords of the graphic design industry. The emphasis on consumer-type brand thinking should therefore not be surprising, nor should the proclivity towards mass media. But, as we have already noted, firms are not populated by consumers. The employee's relationship with their firm is far more profound and complex than a consumer's relationship with a visual brand. As a result, corporate brands do not play the same role. They are simply one manifestation of a more complex reality. Hence, firms assuming that a good graphic job is all it takes is analogous to a banker assuming all it takes is an Armani suit to get a deal. Visual stimuli are important. But more compelling is that web of meaning created by use of language and turn of phrase. 'Logoising' is not the same as having a coherent internal language.

Language is a symbolic method of communication. Abstract ideas are rendered into a visual and spoken code universal to an ethnic community. Language builds on the same visual source of power as graphic identities. But instead of acting as a brand – a signpost – language conveys complex ideas in a form which makes those ideas intelligible to that particular community. In an important sense they define the way of thinking of that group of people. They are the foundation of thought, not a roadmap. They are a medium for ideas as well as a definer of those ideas. In general, the more sophisticated a community's language, the more advanced will be its ideas. Also, perhaps more importantly, the more cohesive that community will be and the more able to export its ideas and approaches to other communities and markets. The community with the richest language will tend to win the battle of global intellectual capital.

While many firms have latched onto the use of corporate branding, few have understood the power of language, and even fewer have evolved their own symbolic lexicons. At the end of the day, the symbols that will drive the cohesiveness of a corporate community, that will make it stand apart, will be its language. As Proust put it, 'Language, not politics is the foundation of a nation.'[1]

---

[1] Proust, Marcel. *Remembrance of Things Past*. Random House, 1982.

Towards unique corporate character

Every modern firm has probably given lip-service to the concepts of values and culture. The real limitation of the values and culture debate is that it is intensely intangible. As a management tool it is utterly ungraspable, unmanipulatable. This is arguably its potential strength – that it is hard for an individual CEO to destroy or create and therefore institutional continuity can be defended against the exigencies of individualism. However, it is a limitation by the same token.

To make the notion of values (or what we have called ethos) meaningful, the concepts have to be articulated. Unless articulated they are no use as a management tool. As we have already discussed, articulating them as a list is meaningless. Once listed they are dead. To be alive they have to form the fabric of everyday interaction – they need to influence relationships.

One of the tools any firm has to articulate its ethos in this living sense is its use of graphical and verbal representation – to turn it into a visual series of prompts. This is a fundamentally trivialised issue in most corporations. Most have mistaken graphical representation of values for an extension of branding – somehow beguiling the constituencies of the firm the same as the marketing department woos the consumer.

Most corporations face the challenge of how to move from brand-oriented identity programmes to evolving a unique language – a language that is adaptable, organic and which is used by employees in their daily interaction. Once again, the firms that appear to have progressed furthest down that road are the people businesses which trade in knowledge. As a result of the importance they place on managing collective knowledge, codifying it and disseminating it in a way that will be valued by clients, they tend to have evolved quite unique languages. McKinsey, for example, has evolved a highly unique (although now widely emulated) set of presentational techniques. This slide-based communications format is tantamount to a language. It conditions the way material is delivered to clients; it conditions

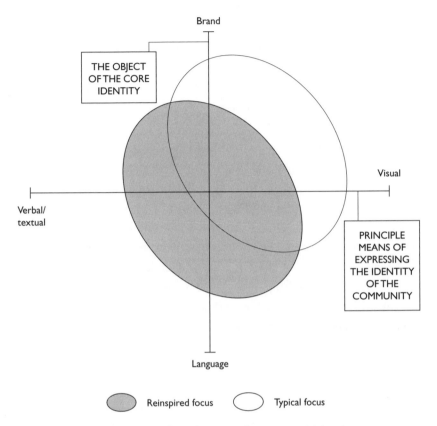

Figure 7.1 **The foundations of reinspired identity**

the way consultants frame their thought-processes. Unless an employee grasps the language they will not be 'in'. At the other end of the people business spectrum, Ogilvy and Mather's Brand Stewardship plays a similar role in unifying the voice of the firm in a way that makes it distinct and admired. Its method of handling client's brands, the language used to articulate the problems and solve them, are all deeply embedded in the community of the firm.

Compare this to another commonly quoted 'values driven' organisation – the UK cosmetics retailer Body Shop. Body Shop has evolved from corporate branding to iconography. The ethos, the positioning of the firm on a number of complex (and dangerous) moral issues is well understood and reflected clearly in both the visual representation but also the external language of the firm. But it has not evolved a proprietary language articulated to the depth of a McKinsey. A McKinseyite is stamped for life. A Body Shop executive could quite innocuously defect to Boots, a venerable if somewhat weary UK rival.

In a forthcoming decade dominated by visual media, propelled by the explosion of the World Wide Web and proliferation of digital channels, it will be overwhelmingly tempting for companies to believe that the only thing that matters is uniform corporate branding; that visual identity will be enough to knit the fabric of the firm together. The company will become a consumer item and the firm's Intranet will become a form of mass media. Hopefully, it is clear that this would be a very limiting mistake. The Internet and e-mail are a medium conducive to the development of a proprietary language. Proprietary language is the surest way to foster a powerful community capable of replicating itself successfully. Language endures. Graphic design dates. Companies die!

8

Path 4: Embedding a shared corporate heritage

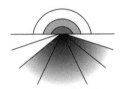

The past as future

Why does the past matter? The past is by definition past, for the reason that the present has overtaken it! Surely the only role it plays is a quaint nostalgia – we may examine the Model T in the motor museum but we sure as hell wouldn't give up our Mondeo for it!

Nostalgia is, of course, one sentimental vein of an essential human yearning. We all need to feel we come from a solid foundation. If we do not have a great pedigree, as few of us have, we try as hard as we can to invent one for future family generations. Our present is often as much about our past as it is about our future. Half the aristocratic titles in the UK were either bought or earned rather than inherited. Having secure origins gives us the confidence to innovate, to push the envelope. They also give us something to fight to preserve for the future. In an important way, our history gives us a purpose. The communities of corporations are no different.

Heritage as defence versus building block

The problem with having a history is that it can be used either positively or negatively. Many firms have tended to use it negatively – to defy change, the same as the British aristocracy. Corporate heritage in this sense – of having a venerable corporate history that confers some sort of superior class, some market right – is a defunct concept. More firms than we can possibly list, from British Leyland in the UK to PanAm in the US, have all had venerable histories and all got slammed by markets evolving faster than them. A rock, even a very venerable one, gets thrown aside by the waves of change.

This received image of heritage is the negative one. It has sprung from the litany of firms who came a cropper primarily in the 1980s and early 1990s because they were convinced that the fact they had been around for a long time meant they had a birthright to occupy a market space. We all know that is an anachronistic mindset.

The positive and fruitful side of heritage comes from a strong sense of social identity. As we have already explored, social identity, the fact of belonging, is a profound human need. Without it we have no means of measuring our success. The point about this type of heritage is that it is not static. It does not say, 'We have been here since 1897, therefore we are owed immortality.' It says we have a shared identity with a lineage, a community, stretching back, and that gives us a solid, unquestionable foundation conferring the authority to push the bounds. There is a history of which we are a part, of which we can feel proud and which we also in turn have the opportunity to shape. The distinction to be drawn is a simple one – it divides between static heritage, 'we did this and therefore . . .' and living heritage, 'we did it once, we know we can do it again and we must do it again . . .'.

Living versus dead heritage

So what constitutes living heritage? What is its texture? At heart, the medium of heritage is perhaps not what you would expect. In its positive manifestations it is not a list of values scribed on ageing, mottled parchment; it is not a museum of prototypes; it is not the dusty tomes of ancient board minutes; it is not enshrined in the cigar-stained oak boardroom; it is not scrupulously preserved logotype or escutcheons. These are the trappings of a dead culture; a firm clinging to the past.

The hallmarks of heritage as defence are not difficult to spot. The bulk of the firm's business will be in the same sector it has always been; the same underlying technology will still be the foundation of the firm's products. The claims to market dominance will be strong. Profitability may be high due to low investment requirements. However, there will be absolute inertia when it comes to fundamental change. The firm will have its way of doing things and that's the end of the story.

By contrast, a living heritage may not look like heritage at all. The original identity may have evolved beyond recognition. The escutcheons of yore will be consigned to attics. All the founder's portraits may have been sold off. The firm may have changed sectors altogether. There may be no dusty credos. The corporate building will probably be new. Indeed, the firm may be relocated in another part of the country altogether.

So, in the face of all this change, how can the community of the firm possibly have a shared heritage? This brings us back to language. Language is the medium of continuity for any community and one of the most powerful expressions of its own continuity is, we would posit, nothing less than story telling.

The power of corporate fable

To a significant degree, a living, evolving heritage is in fact kept alive by nothing more than stories – what one older member of the community communicates about it to a new member. In a broader sense, living history is closely bound up with story telling. Stories bring the past alive, they provide the opportunity to re-craft it in a way that makes it relevant to the present. They also engage and show humour. All the big companies that have thrived over long periods of time are the subject of stories – apocryphal stories about the activities of their founders, of near bankruptcies, of take-overs. These stories will tend to reflect something of the essence of these firms. Whether it's Ford, Apple, Walmart or Microsoft, stories convey the essence of where the community comes from, what it holds dear.

Stories are, of course, ultimately fiction. The act of telling them inevitably involves re-invention, even if the kernel of truth remains. This type of organic history, of evolving heritage which is subject to continual reinterpretation, can be distinctly unsettling for some Boards. This is also true of organic communications environments like Intranets – a natural medium for stories. The first instinct is to control, to prescribe, to police, to fix it to an absolute form, an absolute message whether on CD-Rom or a server, controlled by knowledge managers reporting to a Chief Knowledge Officer. This of course never works. It only serves to weaken the community. Healthy communities are always evolving and their stories evolve with them, but ideally from a strand of continuity, of trustworthy reinterpretation.

The great religions are, of course, founded on story telling. They are all rich in stories and oral traditions which bring their more abstruse teachings and meanings alive. If they have a weakness it is doctrine. People are not motivated by doctrine or abstract ideas of right and wrong. They are motivated by tales of lives to which they can aspire, with which they empathise or which inspire feeling. The process of enactment is a surrogate for living out someone else's life as our own. That is why, behind the dry facts of commercial success, what fascinates us all is the human story – the making of Bill Gates or of John D. Rockefeller.

The golden mean: continuity with change

How does a firm secure its heritage but ensure its continued relevance? To do so, it has to avoid the polarity most firms fall into of shedding heritage altogether or, at the other extreme, hiding behind heritage as an excuse for inaction. One wipes out the foundations of the community which take so many years to lay. The other traps the firm in its own anachronistic cement.

The only process that allows heritage to live and evolve is (principally oral) communication. A healthy, reinspired company is one populated with anecdotes and stories; stories of its foundation, of its heroes and villains. The firm treats itself as a medium. Its ethos is transmitted through the portraits painted in people's minds of the forces that have shaped the firm.

This implies some actions which are fundamentally uncomfortable for many firms. It presupposes an intense level of informal communication, particularly between Board level managers and employees. It also implies a high degree of informal interaction. That is the way heritage is transmitted. It is not principally through glossy brochures subcontracted to an outside consulting firm (although that can be a support process). It is not through painstakingly articulated values statements.

Whatever they may say to the contrary, most firms are intensely uncomfortable with informal communications. Offices are sectioned off. Car spaces differentiate Board and non-Board members. Corporate headquarters tend to be secreted away from the place of operations. The activities of senior executives are highly cloaked. The intense level of M&A which preoccupies much of senior management time takes place behind closed doors, in rooms populated by bankers and lawyers. The personalities, the personal lives, the predilections of these people are a mystery to most employees. The degree of genuine, regular, informal engagement is extremely low indeed. In short, the environment is not conducive to a living heritage. Senior executives do not perceive themselves as having any role in fostering corporate folklore. Nor do they usually see the relevance of doing so.

It is only in the first generation founding stage that fable is commonly used (even if unconsciously) to bind and motivate the community of the firm. Sam Walton was legendary for his avuncular stories about the fruits of good service. The quasi-myths of figures as diverse as Ray Crock of MacDonalds and David Ogilvy of Ogilvy and Mather abound within and beyond the firms they founded. The staged myths of Richard Branson's ballooning exploits infuse the entire organisation of the Virgin Group with an ethos of iconoclastic daring that have inspired it to successfully lay siege to the venerable giant BA. Anita Roddick's determination to 'walk the talk' has buttressed (at least in its home market of the UK) what is a marginal ecological pitch against retail giants such as Boots and Bath and Body Works. Bill Gates' legendary drive continues to electrify what is already the world's most valuable company. The stories that evolve in their wakes constitute an important ingredient of the glue which defines the personal aspiration of many of their employees.

The strategy of heritage

Intelligent people who do not have family escutcheons and country estates to call their own will inevitably look to identify with a community that supplies a past they can have a legitimate claim upon. Being part of such a past is an essential part of feeling good about our present and passionate about our future. We have already talked about the demise of the great social institutions, from the Church through to the local community. Unless web communities really take hold (which has to be as great a fiction as the value of most web businesses!), the only viable institution left is the company. The community of the company will, in our view, become the

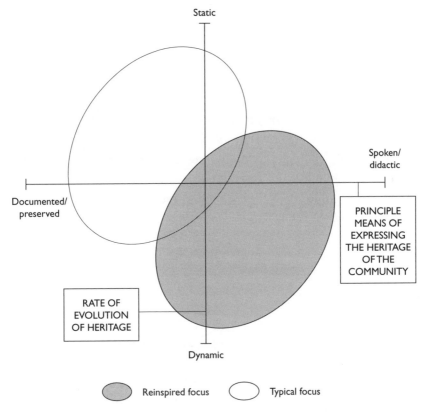

Figure 8.1 The balance of living heritage

focal point of collective identity for most intelligent people. This means those firms that wish to compete for such affection will need to evolve a strategy for satisfying the needs of a community starved workforce.

A vital component of that strategy is cultivating a sense of continuity – a heritage that the core constituents of the company can call their own. This strategy of continuity cannot be about the defence of a preordained stature. It cannot be about resisting change. It will not be founded on any of the bric-à-brac that conventionally designates continuity. To be relevant it has to be continually evolving, adapting and, more importantly, to be used. The only medium that meets these criteria is when heritage is transmitted through anecdote and story. The strategy of continuity is about articulating a grand purpose in the language of everyday events – turning water to wine.

It is the contention of this book that few firms actively manage their heritage and in so doing they forsake a vital ingredient of corporate differentiation. They invite impermanence and are undermined with transience. Again, they all too often mistake corporate logo schemes for meaningful, enduring identity. The key to getting out of the dark conundrum of insecurity is very simple. At heart it boils down to nothing more than communications. This brings us on to the fifth path of reinspiration.

9

Path 5: Releasing the flow of ideas: inspiring the asking of the big questions

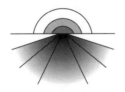

Disruptive resolutions

Introspection is a vital ingredient of spiritual health. We all have to ask ourselves why we are here, what role do we play, and what can possibly come of it all? Firms, like religions, have to allow such questions to be asked and also to respond to them. That is how they secure their relevance as institutions in our lives.

Every great breakthrough is the product of confronting personal and communal despair. It is one of life's paradoxes that we usually have to break in order to mend! The process of asking the difficult questions, of questioning the status quo, is what produces forward movement. Momentum is not the result of a clinical, tightly managed process. It is more usually the output of a somewhat traumatic and heated set of exchanges with ourselves and others.

Central to this process is communication. Intense communication fosters a degree of disruption but also ultimately resolution, typically through the emergence of a new order or approach. It is a process that moves us forward even when it looks as if it will stall things.

What is anathema to this dynamic is the management philosophy of the reengineers. Reengineering seeks to improve performance through a single, one-time change in internal structures. Of course, this ignores the fact that successful change is never one-off. It is continual and rarely clinically controlled or mandated, except in its early stages. A reengineering obsessed firm will never produce break-through ideas; it will not tolerate the communicational richness and fluidity that underlie reinspiration. But, unfortunately, such orderly, controlled and mandatable concepts of change have proved more comfortable for senior managers than the less manageable flow of hard-hitting self-questioning fostered by intense communications.

Communications as strategy

The living culture we discussed in Chapter 8 is predicated on rapid, informal internal communications. Historically, a control-obsessed management has usually impeded that process. Just as for 15 years, up until 1996, the French government had an active policy of policing and preserving the integrity of the French language against the process of Anglicisation, so many firms have tried to lock the door to new, disruptive influences. The dangers of such control have always been clear. In around 1020 AD Canute apocryphally tried to hold back the tide and almost got drowned. In 1995 Barings Bank did not want to face up to its profit dependence on the activities of a rogue trader in Singapore. It went bust.

Even though more enlightened management teams have recog-nised that a healthy, somewhat chaotic internal dialogue is essential to innovation, intuitively control has somehow always been too temping to resist. That is what management is all about, surely? However a management team might persuade itself otherwise, selec-tive deafness usually signifies self-defensive dumbness and impending disaster. Meanwhile, the organisation of course creates its own methods of bypassing the controls, much as a tree will grow around and finally absorb iron railings.

The process of enquiry is an intensely creative one. It allows good ideas to displace bad ones. In essence it constitutes a process of natural idea selection. As such it is the fuel of quantum innovation. Few groundbreaking ideas come to market through solo effort and there is a reason that large firms usually produce the new products – through from Sony's Walkman to Dupont's Lycra. Talented people tend to gravitate to other talented people where they can engage in competitive debate. Individual talent disrupts but, combined with a constructive community dynamic, it also creates.

For a firm to interrogate itself, to ask the tough questions – even if they are apparently disruptive – is only achieved in an environment where communicational flow is relatively unimpeded.

Communications: from control to creativity

Communicational intensity and innovation are closely related phenomena. The first serious user of e-mail was the scientific research community – an intensely collaboratively competitive one which operates as a somewhat chaotic network of independent thinkers. The idea of innovation through free-wheeling interaction and communication is a very alien one to most companies who view the innovation process in a highly structured, departmental manner. The concept of the R&D department, of the innovation group locked in a facility some way from the main area of production, is symptomatic of the desire on the part of senior management to ring-fence the anarchy of the innovation process, to stop it from infecting the stable work flows of the core business.

This paradigm, that preserves the stable core and removes any source of self-questioning, is replicated in the departmental structure of most organisations. Keeping all the marketers together and separate from the production and IT groups ensures that each focuses narrowly on their task at hand and the machine remains in balance. While a hundred years ago departmentalism began as the specialisation of skills, in a contemporary organisation it is also a powerful

method of control. The volume of informal communications tran-
scending the departmental walls is, if well controlled, minimal and
perfunctory.

This paradigm of organisational control has now had its day (even
if some organisations haven't yet smelt the coffee!). Innovation
cannot be the sole demesne of the R&D department. It has to span
marketing, IT, production, sourcing, HR. It is a fundamentally cross-
functional process. Nor is it naturally an organised process. This is
where reengineering gets it all wrong. Inventiveness cannot be mechanistic. Management teams who are beguiled by consultants into
complex, process-driven innovation reviews are being misled. The
best ideas will well up from the informal process of communications
between thoughtful and committed people. That communications
process will tend to be personal and heated – even anarchic. The
necessary precondition is an environment that encourages such
dialogue, that is secure enough to accommodate a degree of chaos
and which provides the infrastructure to allow it to happen – principally communicational infrastructure.

Unless senior management can swallow a degree of chaos, perhaps
beyond their control, then it will never happen. The more profoundly
control-oriented and interventionist a firm is, and the less trust it
places in its people, then the less innovative it is likely to be, even
if its margins, temporarily at least, may be excellent. The fact is that
managers will not be able to resist the augmenting communicational
wave. Those who continue to endeavour to do so will find themselves redundant. The advent of Intranets and e-mail have
fundamentally altered the internal communications networks of all
large companies to the point where the informal process cannot viably
be resisted.

There are those who continue to hold out, of course. Perhaps
most notable are the nationalised European behemoths – such as the
French state-owned enterprises and the Japanese *kereitsu*. Both groups
have a fundamental question mark over their competitiveness. Both
appear to be characterised by a fundamental fear of asking themselves
the tough questions. Strategy, it seems, is solely for the boardroom.

The future is a matter of utter secrecy – supposedly; except from the outside it is clear they are heading for a brick wall or, indeed, have already hit it!

The trade-off most firms face over the next few years is between control and innovation. In the past this dialectic was described as a low cost strategy versus a strategy of differentiation. Differentiation is synonymous with innovation and, as we discussed in Chapter 1, the pace of innovation has never been greater. Rather than being episodic it is now embedded and continual – it is a competitive imperative. On the other side of the equation, the low cost strategy is no longer viable as a unique source of competitive advantage for most firms. Production-intensive activities have mostly shifted offshore and all firms have access to the same offshore labour pools, whether in Taiwan or Mexico. Cost is a hygiene factor, demanding parity. It will not provide long-term competitiveness. The growth of e-commerce is gradually lowering the acceptable cost barrier even further. (But, perhaps more interestingly, it is also placing the focus on branding and consumer differentiation.)

The inevitable shift away from control will require a huge shift in management mindsets, and, as usual with periods of change, it is senior management sentiment and adaptiveness that hold the key to corporate success. Senior managers will have to move away from organisation and departmentalisation – away from their comfortable role as chess-players – to a role as facilitators. Successful firms will be providers of communication infrastructure to motivated, mobile employees in the business of trading ideas and asking questions. They will also have to move away from the endemic use of spies – alias old-style management consultants – to enforce their notions of structure and help plan their moves of the chess pieces. Instead they will have to hire advisors to facilitate communications – a different breed altogether!

Communicating, but with whom?

Ideas are generated through communications, whether face to face or via satellite. Questions mean nothing unless they are posed to other people. The process of asking questions and generating ideas is intensely social. Even if they have their origins in solitary intro-spection, to have power ideas have to be communicated and tested with others. Modern work, facilitated by IT networks, is to a large extent a process of communication. We trade ideas before we trade stuff.

What, then, do most firms view as the role of communications? The bulk of most company's planned communications activity is external – telling the market about its ideas. The global advertising market is worth around $800 billion in billings and if the other 'below-the-line' activities are included such as promotions and direct mail, it reaches as high as $2 trillion. The average fmcg company spends around 8 per cent of its turnover on its external communi-cations activity. Even for firms in sectors which traditionally have not been communications-intensive, such as investment banking or management consulting, the traction of the marketing communi-cations vortex is unavoidable. With the growth in spend, the sophistication of the marketing process has been refined to a neo-science. The service end of the equation, particularly among advertising agencies, has matured into an industry of global scale. The three dominant groups, Interpublic, Omnicom and WPP, are all capitalized above $5 billion and have in excess of a thousand offices in their networks servicing the needs of their clients on a global basis.

So what is wrong with this picture? The external communications process is an endeavour to get existing and potential buyers of a product or service to believe they need more of it by playing on their emotions. Hundreds, thousands of voices are clamouring to make themselves heard in print and across the air-waves and to embed the imprint of their brand in the head of their audience. This feat is getting harder and harder for the advertiser to achieve. To cut through the deafening babble firms have to spend ever larger amounts of share-holders' cash to achieve an acceptable 'share of voice'.[1] The inflation of mainstream media prices for the past ten years has accentuated most firms' discomfort with this process. Channel proliferation; the maturation of on-line media; the proliferation of new magazine titles – all these things are accelerating the fragmentation and therefore declining effectiveness of mass media. The result is people are ever tougher to reach and require far more precision in terms of messages and targeting. The headache deepens. Spend goes up. Competitive firms are caught in a 'Prisoner's Dilemma'.

This traditional mass-market communications paradigm presumes there is no interaction with the consumer other than through an embodiment of the essence of a product called the brand. As long as the brand is well communicated and the product sound, that is that. The relationship of the firm and customer is arm's length, conducted through a sort of holy ghost intermediary.

This clinical model of the relationship between firm and customer is, of course, shifting dramatically. One key driver of the change is the increasing service component of most products. At the most basic level, the majority of products now carry warranties. If a customer calls the warranty in, a communications event occurs with the company. One expression of the growing level of interaction between the company and customer is the massive growth of the call centre. With the growth of on-line retail and direct order, and the disappearance of the role of the intermediary, the intensity of direct interaction between the firm and its public are increasing dramatically. Suddenly the corporation is very visible. There is little doubt who is behind the product brand. The firm is not the invisible hand it once was.

What does this all mean? Suddenly the corporation has to worry about managing a more intimate, a more interactive relationship with its customers. Relationship marketing is a really tough, unsettling

---

[1] Share of voice is a firm's share of total competitor advertising spend in the category.

challenge. We've all heard the hype but how after all does the firm really personalise and manage its interaction with its customer base? Most firms have intuitively tried to fend off the impending issue by shifting from brand communications to corporate communications – the same bag of tricks but a different object. But there is no avoiding the bold facts – the key suddenly becomes the ability and willingness of the firm's employees to engage in that process. It is no longer a matter of how hot the ad agency is. It is about how engaged employees are.

This is nothing new of course. What is new, however, is the degree to which it is now a blindingly obvious imperative. So, in this new context, is it the right thing to do to spend millions on advertising when what matters in at least equal measure is the level of drive among employees to engage in a relationship with customers? Perhaps, just perhaps, the communications machine is pointing the wrong way?

Internal communications: the last untapped market

The internal communications audience for all companies is, we would assert, at least as important as the external audience. It is an extraordinary fact that many firms don't even have a formal internal communications process. The aggregate spend on internal communications is less than 1 per cent of the spend on external communications!

The reinspired corporation views the internal communications process with as much gravity as it does the external communications process. It recognises that sustaining the ethos of the company and achieving emotional buy-in to its community requires a continual refreshing of the relevance of the firm to its employees. It recognises that the intensity of this communications process, of institutionalised self-questioning, will also drive the level of innovation. Is this the same as Joseph Goebbels-type corporate propaganda? No. It differs fundamentally from external communications in that it is not a one-way flow. Nor is it rigorously structured. It is a dialogue that crosses hierarchical and departmental lines. It is facilitated by shared infrastructure. But otherwise it is free-wheeling. Opinion expressed constructively carries no penalty.

The internal communications process is a complex one and requires more sophistication than the external communications process. There are usually some significant impediments to even starting it on the right footing. If the firm has a formalised internal communications process it will tend to be in the hands of the human resources group. The HR departments of most companies, where they haven't been whittled away completely, tend (with some notable exceptions) not to be populated by the most scintillating communicators. HR is typically geared to administering remuneration structures and promotion policy. It also focuses on doers not thinkers. The classical communications outputs are somewhat dated internal brochures, in-house magazines and a bunch of other hardcopy that often resembles something out of (dare we say it?) a second-rate provincial paper. In other words, it is run by the wrong people – people whose principal skill is not communications. Internal communications is about creating an emotional bond to a shared goal. It is not classical HR.

Interestingly, as the importance of internal communications begins to gather pace, there is an increasing tendency to look upon it as a marketing event. The growing buzz-phrase is 'internal marketing'. And, of course, the people wanting to co-opt the process into their domain are our friends from the marketing department. That they should wish to do so is not exactly surprising – the budgets are beginning to grow and with them the prestige and power control the process confers, particularly since the ultimate provider of content tends to be the CEO!

Control of the internal communications process by the marketing group alone often (although there are important exceptions) is no more healthy than management by its old patrons, the HR department. While internal communications can learn something from the nature of branding at the heart of the external communications process, employees differ from customers in a fundamental way in terms of their relationship with the company. Simply telling someone who has worked in the firm for five years how great it is won't cut much ice.

The second limitation is the proscribed concept of what constitutes communications in the first place. As we have already explored, external communications is becoming less a paper- or TV-based, one-way transmission of information and more an ongoing two-way interaction through a multiplicity of channels, some personal, others impersonal. The same is even more true of internal communications. The way people in a company get to hear things is not through reading second-rate hardcopy pumped out by the publicity department. It is through a process of word of mouth, incidental anecdotes, rumour, story. The phrase that best describes this diffused communicational process is 'network communications'.

The real web: network communications

Network communications means the transmission of ideas and concepts through personalised and fragmented means. All firms have networks – indeed, they have many different networks. Some of these will be formalised, for example, a specific collaborative mechanism to link the marketing and R&D group, enshrined in monthly meetings or team briefings. Other networks will be informal, cutting across departments and even running between the firm itself and its external partners. These informal networks will almost certainly be much more powerful than any formal network the firm may have instituted. They will be the source of most people's information about what is really happening in the firm. They will probably carry much more credence than formal communications channels pumping out the party line.

The basic mistake firms often make is trying to supersede or control these informal channels with a formal communications process.

It never works. Informal communications networks are by their nature personalised and fragmented. They are almost impossible to control. The tale of the boss insisting rumour be stamped out only to be overrun by it, is not apocryphal. The mistake is underestimating what a crucial driver of internal opinion such channels can be. That's how revolutions start. The endemic failure to understand the nature of the rumour-mill is extraordinary, particularly given most executives have now learnt the importance of harnessing PR in their external communications.

And things are set to get better! The growth of IT networks has ushered in probably the single biggest change to corporations in the past 20 years. Not only has it influenced the nature of a firm's relationships with its external audiences, it has fundamentally altered the power of internal networks. There has been an explosion in the penetration of Intranets, first using proprietary software such as Lotus Notes and, more recently, web-based technologies. This has ushered in a complete revolution in the way employees communicate with each other across both departments and geographies. In essence, it has acted to reinforce and amplify the informal networks that already existed. The ability of senior management to control the flow of information between employees is now absolutely non-existent. Such networks cannot be policed.

Before the advent of networked computing and Intranets, a firm's databases were simply a digital version of the library. Whether they resided on CD-ROM, floppy disk or in databanks on the mainframe, the social utility of them was not markedly different from the old-fashioned library. Sure, access was faster and the search process swifter. But several key characteristics had not changed. Access to the data was restricted to an on-demand basis. The file or disk had to be tracked down, permission gained and the data scanned. Second, the process of compilation and updating was a formal one, done by a person employed to fulfil this task. This meant that the process of updating data was necessarily slow and always lagging actuality. So what if it existed in bits and not atoms. It made no fundamental difference to the user.

Technology has changed that paradigm in the past three years. The company can locate the critical databases on the company's server and, with the judicious use of passwords, those data suddenly become instantly accessible to anyone with a PC in the company. Not only that but again, with the judicious use of access protocols, external parties can also be networked into the firm's information infrastructure or Extranets. Strategic suppliers and key customers can all be linked into common database access as well as logistics support. Updating can be real-time.

But, although technology has changed, on the whole psychology has not. In essence, the on-line environment is viewed by most firms as a shared library resource to render the process of data share more efficient. The usual emphasis of Intranets is on formerly paper-based items such as internal directories and address books. Typically, firms construct databases of information such as customer leads, presentational materials, etc., and make them web-enabled. They may appoint knowledge managers to police the process of replenishment and help organise the on-line environment. They may even designate a Chief Knowledge Officer to act as a locus of authority through the inherently anarchic sprawl of the average on-line domain.

However, while firms may establish a reasonably coherent database environment, the relevance of it to the average employee tends to be low. After an initial flush of enthusiasm, the rate of organic replenishment tends to fall away rapidly. Over time the relevance of the information becomes poorer and poorer; utilisation falls. The CIO is left with a system into which cash has been poured which is not used as it should be and which can demonstrate no concrete rate of return. As soon as markets turn down the budget gets squeezed and the downward cycle of irrelevance is self-reinforcing.

This is not to say that the internal IT network is redundant *per se*. Far from it. What is pretty much misconceived is the attempt to co-opt it as a formal knowledge management and dissemination medium. Meanwhile, behind the scenes, informal networks do what they always do – grow exponentially by commandeering whatever means they can to enhance the rate of information exchange. The advent of Intranets and Extranets has in fact been an unprecedented boon for informal communicational networks.

Assuming such networks cannot be eradicated successfully, the second big mistake most firms make with their internal communications processes is not to exploit them. If they understand them at all, most firms have co-opted internal communications networks merely for tactical objectives. The explosion of internal communications activity over the past few years has mostly been a corollary of the process of downsizing/restructuring/reengineering/consolidation. There may be a few months of communications to win support for a proposed merger and then a year-long campaign to achieve buy-in. The following year it all focuses on persuading employees that the productivity drive to deliver on the promises of the deal is in their interests. The accumulation of tactical internal communications events can, if not managed properly, quickly result in one thing – cynicism and then indifference. The internal web-pages get dismissed as a voice-piece for a management wanting to indoctrinate the oppressed victims of yet another restructuring that will release bounteous stock option packages for the top dogs.

From knowledge to chat: the great content issue

By far the most common on-line application is e-mail, not database access or use of the complex, engineered content that populates most corporate Intranets. The interesting thing about e-mail-based communications is that is tends to cross departmental and hierarchical boundaries better than any other medium, principally because it is personal rather than formal. The PC is a highly personal item for most executives – housing personal files and addresses. The great thing about an e-mail message is that it downloads directly onto this personal medium. While a secretary might check it on behalf of their boss, their willingness to review it as a gatekeeper will be lower. Nor is it subject to editing like normal formal content.

Of course, controlling this flow of unedited interaction is probably even harder than controlling informal meetings and telephone conversations. A company not wishing to encourage a marketing group in one division to speak to that in another, or a consulting firm wishing to maintain 'Chinese walls' between teams, can resort to physically locating them in different buildings or even geographies. Their web-enabled data will be protected with passwords and fire-walls. But with e-mail this is irrelevant. The personal communications will flow regardless. Chat will grow exponentially.

Chat-rooms, or the domains where chat is facilitated, are nothing more than a digitised version of the social gathering. However, because they don't require physical presence, they have the additional benefit of being semi-impersonal. They offer the best of both fundamental psychological needs – the desire to communicate, and transact with other people in an informal setting and the desire to retain a degree of anonymity – not to expose all one's warts. As a result, they have shown explosive growth. The organic, accretive content created by these interactions almost certainly exceeds the gigabytes of memory taken up by designed content on most firm's servers. They represent real living knowledge.

But what does such chat have to do with knowledge creation? All the academic talk of the past three years has been about knowledge creation and management; about the virtue of digitised matter. Knowledge in this thesis is equated with storage, filtering and dis-semination of collective information. But what is the relevance of knowledge sitting on CD-ROMS or servers? Knowledge is created by intelligent people in a company engaging in debate. It is no longer live knowledge when stored on a server. At that point it is dead and fixed, like a butterfly collection. The prevalent concept of knowledge management is not the breakthrough idea it is made out to be. It mis-describes reality. The dominant use of IT networks by employees is for a form of information exchange that is essentially social in nature. It cannot be called 'knowledge exchange'. That is too im-personal and pseudo-scientific. It is better termed 'idea trading' or 'chat'. In essence there is nothing new about it, except it can now occur more widely, more readily and therefore information will inevitably get transmitted at a much higher rate. It is the social phenomenon that matters, not the pipeline – the inescapable informal network which characterises the whole of social organisation from the village upwards.

The strategy of chat

So what about the reinspired corporation? The reinspired corporation does not talk about knowledge management. It will talk about the management of a shared sense of commitment to a common purpose. It won't talk about digital databases deployed on servers. It will talk about how to use the informal communications networks of the company to trade ideas as aggressively as possible. It will focus on provoking debate, not controlling it. It will accommodate the continual questioning of the status quo. It will spend substantially on supporting the necessary infrastructure but will not police it as an asset. Senior management will use the system to prod and cajole. The dialogue will at times be heated and widespread. But through it all will run a vein of shared language, analogy and idiom that will save it from incoherence. It will not be a babble but a river.

The internal communications process is one of the most powerful tools in the armoury of the reinspired corporation. Using it successfully for purposes of invoking long-term commitment to the development of the company requires getting four things right. First, it must be founded on the use of the informal network and not principally on a structured, classical communications process. Such a network of course needs the right infrastructure, which is no mean feat. Second, it cannot be the management domain of a single department such as HR or, indeed, Marketing. Just as its medium is an informal communicational network, so its owners have to be a broad group of people sharing a common ideology. Again, we come back to our religious analogy. Faith needs evangelists not police. Third, despite being composed of a babble of interactions, to be cohesive,

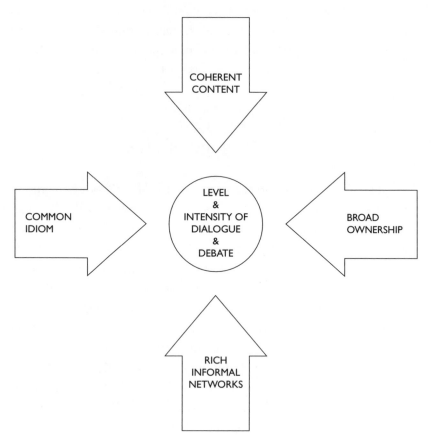

Figure 9.1 The elements of effective internal communications

communications need to be bound together by common language, iconography and idiom as we discussed in Chapter 7. Otherwise communication becomes fractious and tribalised. A strong community needs to speak the same language, even on-line. Finally, it needs content. Therein lies the real challenge. Does the firm actually have anything to say that employees want to hear? Is it capable of writing the equivalent of Bill Gates' *The Road Ahead*?

So where should we turn for living examples? The most enlightened practitioners of networked communications are, once again, the professional services firms.[2] Not surprisingly, it is the same firms that thrive on encouraging their employees to trade ideas, demand the toughest questions of their clients and who expose all their employees to high levels of peer evaluation, that also place most emphasis on internal communications. The process of interrogation and dialogue drives intellectual innovation. That is why firms such as Andersen Consulting have grown at an average of 30 per cent for the past decade. Once again, we have to rethink the benchmarking process – to follow the trail of chat from the top MBA schools. And they ain't talking about industrial firms at HBS or Insead!

---

[2] See Scott, Mark C. *The Intellect Industry; Profiting and Learning from Professional Services Firms.* John Wiley & Sons, 1998.

10

Path 6: Invoking an aspirational view of the collective future

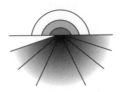

The power of thinking positive

We all want to move forward, to better ourselves. If we have lost that quality we will be resigned, morbid. But few of us are in the position that we can realise our ambitions alone. Life is not a Finals exam completed in solitary silence. We need to be part of a community that will help us fulfil ourselves. Gratification of mature ambitions is fundamentally social. We wish to be seen to have contributed and excelled at those deeds the community values. This need for endorsement we all share, whether we are a knowledge worker or shop floor mechanic.

The concept of social contribution to a community is one that is overlooked by most modern management literature. Senior managers have adopted the motivational language of shareholders – principally focused on economic outputs. This is usually expressed in terms of growth and share price appreciation. 'We will get to forty dollars a share if it kills us.' These lofty corporate aspirations are, on the whole, of little meaning to most employees. Even if they hold stock options or shares, the appreciation of the stock will not be a principal driver of meaning in their lives (unless of course it is an e-business!).

The conventional and ubiquitous definition of progress in terms of metrics such as share price and sales fundamentally misses the emotional point. To feel good about themselves, most people require to feel that they are contributing to building something admirable. The goal is not abstract. It is connected with gaining admiration and social respect. Money is simply a hygiene factor or a by-product.

Share-price focused managements also tend to misconstrue that the only thing that matters to people is personal accomplishment. Most people are personally ambitious. But the most fundamental expression of that ambition is to win the admiration and also the affection of those around them. We are going somewhere and we are getting there together. Again, the motive is fundamentally social in nature. This is why team sports are so compelling. The heroes they produce are the product of group success.

Many firms have lost touch with these fundamental aspects of positiveness. The only goal is EPS growth – a financial metric that few people in the firm will understand, let alone believe in. Failure to espouse a positive sense of direction starves the aspirations of managers and employees. Watching institutional shareholders and Board members reap fortunes from the stock price is not a positive sense of direction. It is a slow form of de-motivation.

From strategy to aspiration

To convince a group of people that the future is worth fighting for, an organisation needs to know where it is going. Knowing where you are going is synonymous in contemporary business think with corporate strategy – if you have a strategy you are likely to make headway. Ever since the publication of Michael Porter's hugely influential *Competitive Advantage*, most management literature has taken up 'strategy' as its mantra. Strategy means having a place to go and a roadmap to get there. Most CEOs if pressed would naturally claim they have a strategy. They might even employ a Director of Strategy to reinforce the point (although that odd position is often something of a non-position). The argument would follow that without a strategy, no one would know what island the ship was sailing towards next.

The goal of most modern corporate strategy is, as we have already mentioned, to maximise shareholder returns. That means maximising cashflow which, when discounted back to its present value, will produce the enterprise value of the firm. Few managers, let alone employees, will be able to define cashflow as an accounting term. They will certainly not know how to calculate an NPV for their business. It is an intensely abstract concept for most people. If we turn back to the analogy of a crew motivated to pull harder on the yard arms to reach the fabled Caribbean isle all the quicker, the goal of EPS growth would be akin to the same sailors sweating away as part of an experiment to test the aerodynamics of gaff-rigged sails – it is not compelling.

Corporate strategy, which takes enterprise value as its cue, tends to presuppose that an organisation is a dead, lumpen mass to be melded in senior management's hand like a piece of putty. That attitude comes through again and again in interviews with the 'star' managers. It is an attitude propagated by old-style management consultants and bankers. Enterprise value based strategy (more recently acceded by EVA[1]) easily forgets the people and what motivates those people.

As discussed in Chapter 5, corporate strategy is wildly over-rated in importance – even if EPS enhancement could be called strategy! Actually most large organisations are not guided by formal strategy at all. They are guided by a long-term organisational drive. At its most abstract, firms, like organisms, have an organic objective of growth and propagation. In essence this urge replicates on a collective scale the impulse of its more influential members to expand their own horizons and exercise the ambit of their egos. And that is a good thing.

---

[1] See Bennett, S. Stewart III, and Stern, Joel M. *The Quest for Value: The EVA Management Guide.* Harper Business, 1987.

At heart, strategy should be about influencing the organic evolution of a living entity. Part of that process is allowing the organisation to form a sense of what it aspires to achieve, what direction it is heading in, what fruits it has to reach for. And this aspiration has to be emotionally powerful enough that employees can believe in it. No employee will believe with any conviction in EVA! They have to be able to visualise the next island of landfall and its prospective delights. Setting the course needs good management, as does setting expectations. But if the vision is clear enough and compelling enough, bright people will have a wonderful habit of finding the inner resources to fight for it, even if the path is stony and obstructed (although preferably not internally!). The priority therefore is articulating that vision, framing the aspiration.

The founder gospel phenomenon

So how does a firm find that inspiring sense of direction? A few firms seem to have inculcated a tremendously positive sense of orientation – in some cases almost verging on evangelism. Bill Gates' well articulated *Road Ahead*, Richard Branson's endless daredevil endeavours, from ballooning to assaulting the insurance industry, Goizueta's quasi-crusading objective of putting a Coke within everyone's reach – all stand out from the pack as imbuing their firms with an evangelistic sense of mission. All, of course, have had the benefit of a semi-mythical leader driving the pace. But the process is not necessarily so personalised in other cases. A number of Japanese firms in the mid-1980s – Sony, Mitsubishi, Toyota – seemed to be gripped by an expansionist zeal which electrified their conquest of the US market. But, of course, the number of examples is limited. Most firms are gripped by an introverted obsession with strategy, few by an expansionist sense of mission.

The power of shared positivism is probably best illustrated by the phenomenal growth of successful start-ups. The example of the

Internet stars such as Yahoo and Amazon.com stand in stark contrast to the fate of industrial behemoths like ITT and Hanson plc, both of which now have smaller market caps. The collective enthusiasm of people contributing to the birth of a company inspires them to great acts. At a broad level it is a function of emotional involvement – close personal identification with the goals of the community. These firms tend to be far less obsessive and anally retentive. They have a product or service idea, and a market to conquer. Established companies, by contrast, tend to lack that exhilarating clarity. They navel-gaze – employing consultants and other corporate therapists to diagnose their angst and inertia. In some respects it is analogous to the difference between youth and middle age. The trick of course is to be a Picasso!

The question is, how do established, long-standing firms replicate the same energy of their youthful counterparts? Thirty years into a marriage, how is the stimulus re-sparked? The same question dogs every institution in its middle years, through from marriage to corporate management. The failure to find a satisfactory answer from within is almost certainly why the answer is so often thrust upon the community from without. Whether in the form of an aggressive LBO team or a driven 'green-mailer', assets without energy will be seized by those that still have it, the same as stalled marriages seem inexorably to deteriorate into a mire of affairs.

Most firms in that position have one answer – to hire a new CEO and institute a turn-around – back to asset-based, tactical strategy. It is akin to having to resort to surgery when what mattered in the first place was long-term preventative health management. But, if it is not just about the CEO, where do firms find their aspirational energy?

Role models as an energy source

Employees need to have a clear sense about where they are going – what rewards the company holds if they are to invest themselves fully in it. Financial reward systems are one tool; promotion mech-anisms are another; evaluation methodologies are the natural accompaniment of them. These are all tools; they are not the foun-dation of what we have called positive aspiration. Innumerable books have been written about honing these tools, so rather than repeat them, let us focus on the foundation – the cordite that will propel the firm forward and which is a source of reinspiration. For, we would argue that in the absence of this source of energy, no reward or evaluation system, however good, will truly differentiate the firm's performance.

The most powerful means to animate an end game is to have heroes. Heroes create compelling identification. They also create goals which are tangible. Hitting productivity scores of 3 Delta or sales per customer of $X000 or similar metric goals work only to a degree. But they suffer from the abstraction we have already talked about. Because of their prescriptiveness they also erode inventiveness and tend to lead to exhaustion and with exhaustion their efficacy declines yet further. They have that neurotic smack of control that saps optimism.

Role models are very different. They embody achievement in a form that can be emulated. They breathe and live. They inspire emotional fascination. That is why when asked, many successful entrepreneurs will quote their inspiration as being another individual. They won't put it down to a great stock option scheme. That is why we are so compelled by great explorers, discoverers of islands, people of intense moral courage that raise the bar and invite us to admire those that follow.

Most firms have eliminated the role model and replaced it with numeric targets. They are more manageable, their relationship to bottom-line performance is clear and they can be imposed uniformly across an entire organisation. Perhaps the most refined (and thank-fully balanced) of them all is the Balanced Scorecard. But how turned on does your average employee get about a balanced scorecard or a 360° evaluation form?

People need to know that if they subscribe wholeheartedly to a community endeavour that they will become more like the person they have always craved to be. They need to see the acknowledgement and endorsement it will deliver. If you list the firms that have done extraordinarily well over the last decade they will have strong heroes. Like the corporate language we examined in Chapter 7 and the story telling we discussed in Chapter 8, role models bring intangible objectives alive. And it is only when they are alive that they are relevant. This is partly why professional services firms have inexorably drawn the best and brightest – joiners can identify with the partner-heroes as models of personal aspiration.

The path of emulation is exactly the path of the Great Religions. They are replete with stories and each story has its hero, from the humble peasant that holds steadfast to their belief, to the most illustrious prophet. The religions tend to embody abstract concepts of right and wrong in the specific parable of one individual's trial of faith. By making them human and fallible, they do not require vast intellect to be understood. They require empathy – something each of us relies on to form our view of others.

The strategy of aspiration

We have posited a revolution – although quietly. That strategy is not as important as aspiration. That aspiration cannot be nurtured by the usual tactical tools of reward schemes and evaluation procedures (although they of course have their role to play), nor solely by top management charisma. To be harnessed as a powerful tool, aspiration has to be made to live. One way to achieve that is by setting up role models to guide aspiration. These figures do not solely reside at the top. They should exist at all levels of the organisation. An organisation of home-bred, accessible heroes will be a high performance community. The object of ambition will be clear and the habits necessary for success will be there to be emulated.

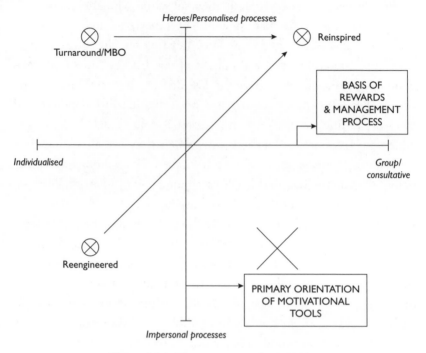

Figure 10.1 The strategy of aspiration

What such an approach implies is that managers throughout the organisation can no longer view their role as simply gatekeepers or controllers. They have to see their role as setting a motivating example. In such a community, management is no longer management. Nor is it evangelism. It is education by example.

11

Path 7: Cultivating corporate mystique

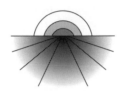

The power of collective myth

Myth, and its close relation mystery (that which cannot be readily explained), are closely bound up with aspiration. And aspiration, as we have explored, is a foundation of growth. We all long to understand what we do not quite understand. Since we do not understand it, and we do not have access to it, we will tend to think more of it than we otherwise would. It is a fundamental characteristic of our natural curiosity. We admire and strive for what is slightly beyond our grasp.

The power of myth is nothing new – the Greeks mastered it 3000 years ago! But what is with few exceptions unappreciated is the role of myth in the corporate world. Goldman Sachs in banking, KKR in private equity, McKinsey in consulting, Disney in entertainment, Microsoft in IT, LVMH in luxury consumer goods, Berkshire Hathaway in fund management – each have a mythical status which influences the degree of revered envy in which they stand, the energy with which bright young people clamour to be admitted to the club, and the commitment of those who are already insiders or shareholders.

Myth not only attracts customers seeking to identify with an admired entity, it more importantly drives the power of the community of the firm. The more value emotionally pertaining to being an insider, the stronger the organisation. Myth is an important reinforcer of the value of being in rather than out. An ex-McKinsey consultant will regard the McKinsey network as among her most important for the rest of her working life. An ex-Goldman's banker commands respect through borrowed mystique and will always have recourse to it. The same cannot be said of many firms. Few firms have the strength of networks these communities enjoy – and, let's not forget, it is the relationship network that will be one of the key drivers of a firm's competitiveness in the next millennium.

Image versus myth

Firms are increasingly careful to manage their 'image'. Most major firms retain PR specialists to ensure they get the right coverage in the press. An increasing number have switched advertising dollars from supporting their individual consumer brands to reinforcing their corporate brands. Corporate brand advertising now constitutes around 15 per cent of ad dollars compared to 5 per cent in 1982. In the process their corporate brands have been massaged, repositioned and polished. Again, this brings us back to our discussion of the limitations of brands. Brands are an effective means to create an emotional bond with consumers. An employee's relationship with a firm is fundamentally different and far more complex. If this relationship is managed through brands, it is no relationship at all.

What matters to intelligent employees is that there is value in being in rather than out. Myth, not branding, is a far better expression of the value of participation. Brands are signposts; myth is a half-perceived place beyond the signposts, accessible to only a few. Being part of that place, reaching it, is the beginning of a special relationship between firm and employee. This same phenomenon has been true of all the world's great institutions, from the Knight's

Templars, to the House of Lords, to the CIA! But what very few firms do is to harness the power of myth.

Myth versus secrecy

Although easily mistaken for one another, myth and secrecy are not the same thing. One is inclusive and expansionist, the other defensive and exclusive. Like good and evil, they are two sides of the same coin. Interestingly, despite the reams of data they pump out, most firms are intensely secretive about their decision-making. Corporate strategy is kept to the boardroom. M&A activity is hush-hush. The number of real insiders is small – usually limited to board-level management. This sort of secrecy is not conducive to mystique. It is exclusive to top management. It creates a division between internal outsiders and insiders and, as such, is divisive. It foments politics and fragmentation, not union. A powerful organisation is not divided; it is unified and differentiated in its unity.

Most firms that think they have evolved a level of mystique have done nothing more than taken pleasure in tormenting everyone else with their tightly guarded secrets. In a networked environment such secrecy is a hopeless vanity. Company 'secrets' will leak out if the company is divisive and secretive – that is the way of such things. This will almost certainly not happen to the same degree if the firm has a strong community cloaked in its own fruitful myth. The corporate police will be redundant but the crown jewels will be safe. Everyone will have an interest in protecting them.

Opacity versus transparency

Most contemporary corporate improvement initiatives are based on simplification and increased transparency. A key driver of this push for simplification and intelligibility has been the core competencies crusade. It has been matched by an increasing volume of corporate communications to the investor community. The bulk of a modern corporation's communications is, of course, directed at customers and shareholders. Increasingly, with the growth of on-line media, it is aimed at exposing the 'friendly face' of the company – dropping the kimono.

This type of consumer-oriented transparency has its costs. It fundamentally reduces the cachet of being inside versus out – the divide is shortened and even bridged. With it myth fades and comparative shopping – known by consultants melodramatically as benchmarking – becomes the order of the day. It is fundamentally a customer-oriented approach, whether these customers are investors, consumers or clients. It is not an employee-driven strategy.

We would posit that there is far too great a concern for clarity by most top managers, particularly promoted by certain groups of management consultants with their simplified paradigms. This is not to say that it can or should be avoided – the vast availability of data and other research on-line makes that impossible. But nor should it be mistaken for a source of competitive advantage. The more clearly a firm is understood does not mean the more accurately it will be valued or be able to create value.

Contrary to the thrust of much of contemporary business thinking, there is much evidence to suggest that a degree of opacity has decisive benefits. It means access to the club is restricted. Being an insider as either an investor or employee bestows unusual benefits. Berkshire Hathaway's shareholder meetings, for example, have the enigma of a Masonic gathering. Reflect back on the concurrence of events that drove five hundred plus souls to drag the Sarsens to Stonehenge. It may sound far-fetched, but the myth of what they were doing must have been a real motivator. Participation in a myth is an intensely social fulfilment.

The strategy of myth versus the myth of strategy

So how does a firm cultivate myth to its competitive advantage? The first pitfall to avoid is the assumption that a firm can advertise its way to admiration. Advertising is good for brands. But it does little for corporate mystique. The way myth evolves is, once again, through informal relationship networks. The key for the corporation is allowing those networks to evolve as richly as possible, like the root structure supporting the tree. The more cohesive the network, the more enduring will be its membership. The more embedded its language, the more the firm will stand apart. The network will span both those currently employed and those that have moved on. As the network strengthens, so the myth will strengthen with it.

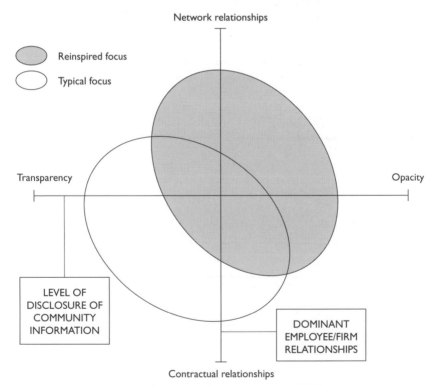

Figure 11.1 The strategy of myth

Once again, industrial and service firms have much to learn from those businesses whose competitive advantage is solely founded on the intellectual talent of their people – professional services firms. The myth attached to firms such as McKinsey and Goldman Sachs begins from the day graduates compete to become insiders. They are recruited by role models, by senior professionals, not by a grey, disinterested member of some HR group. They are inculcated in the language, in the aspirations of the firm, not regaled with a diatribe about rules and corporate history. The informal network begins from day one. It continues even when they leave. McKinsey's post-McKinsey network is legendary and closely cultivated. Its mystique spreads through its ambassadors. No industrial or service firm this author can think of replicates the same web of fraternity as these professional services businesses.

By contrast, industrial and service firms tend to be vessels in which talented people temporarily travel. They do not define the journey itself. They mistake capital – the ship – for the source of their competitive advantage. A firm's competitive advantage is all really in the crew!

12

The shape of the reinspired corporation: towards a new dawn

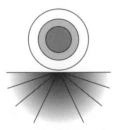

From steel, silicon and cash to brains, flesh and blood

Large businesses are nothing more than a web of relationships – relationships between employees, customers, suppliers and even shareholders. The business is not an impersonal construct. It is not an asset. It is fundamentally personal and organic. This proposition flies in the face of the host of asset-oriented value-management techniques that drive contemporary management thinking, through from fundamental concepts of corporate strategy to cash-based valuation.

Ironically, no term is now more widespread than 'relationship marketing'. However, in this new hierarchy of priorities, the employee tends to come a resounding second in terms of the energies focused on inculcating their commitment. The key audience of relationship marketing is the consumer – the outsider. Every firm under the sun has made it a strategic priority to become customer facing.

It does not take a rocket scientist to point out that this is a major failure of logic. The dominant driver of a customer's experience of the firm is ever increasingly its people. In the past a product was simply sold anonymously. There would be a consumer brand – such as the Taurus – and the customer need not concern themselves with the corporation behind it. They would probably never have contact with the corporation and not care about it. The important thing was the quality of the product and the power of the consumer brand. This is changing fast.

The role of service is increasing rapidly and the service content of most products is increasing exponentially. The proportion of value added derived from this part of the value chain is increasing even faster. In this new world of intense interface between the customer and the firm, the role of the employee is perhaps more visible than it has ever been before. Whether it be through call centres or as a result of the increased customisation of products, the old barriers between internal and external are falling fast.

Along with the increasing human component of goods and services, the basis of competitive advantage is, not surprisingly, shifting in the same direction. The only viable strategy for most firms is differentiation and differentiation is acutely dependent on the combined skills and drive of employees. It all comes back to the same thing – flesh and blood.

On this dimension most firms are lamentably lacking in a 'strategic' approach. The crowning obsession of most senior management teams continues to be playing the chess game of tradable assets under a set of rules called corporate strategy. As hopefully we have argued forcibly, corporate strategy no longer deserves to occupy good minds to the degree it does. It is fundamentally tactical. What really matters is the strength of the community, the cohesion of its shared ethos, and the ardour of the will to replicate that is driving it. It is about inspiration – an entirely emotional matter.

The way to secure a powerful community is to have a strong moral framework, where individual priorities are satisfied through group objectives, where there is a unifying and unique shared language, where a fabric of stories keeps the flame of heritage alive, where exchange of ideas and dialogue is intense (even to the point of self-questioning), although always within a context of positive ambition for self-betterment and where membership of the club confers a status

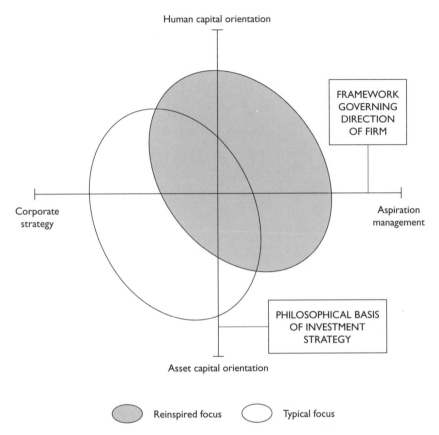

Figure 12.1 **From corporate strategy to reinspiration**

no one would willingly or rationally forgo. The firm that has these characteristics will be unstoppable and will enjoy that dream of all organisations and organisms alike – longevity. It might even be able to build the corporate equivalent of a Chartres that will still inspire awe and admiration almost eight centuries later.

For the sceptical – for the controllers, for the old-school accountants – it is worth remembering that the laws of reinspiration have a good pedigree. The Great Religions each have a greater market share (or share of mind and soul) than any company will ever secure – even Coke, GE and Microsoft combined. This book has skipped

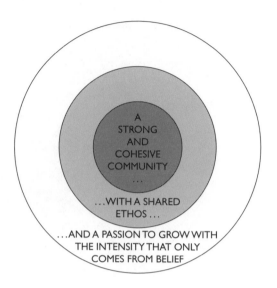

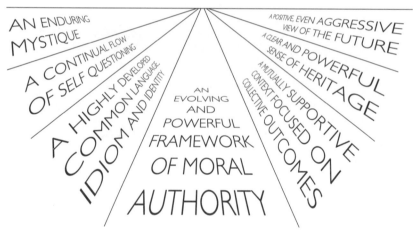

Figure 12.2 The reinspired corporation

fleetingly over the lessons they hold but closer examination (if you choose to undertake it) will simply reinforce the point. The reinspiration model is disarmingly simple. But it requires real management guts to put it to work. The best non-religious models are not the usual ones – they are professional service firms, alias 'people businesses' – which have all but been ignored by the mainstream consultants. We would posit that the art of benchmarking needs to be rewritten!

Charles Gatton Darwin in his book *The Next Million Years* suggested almost 50 years ago that to make a sizeable impact on the human species an individual leader will have three choices – direct political action, change the genetic composition of the human species or create a creed. He concludes that 'a creed gives the best practical hope that man can have for really controlling his future fate.'[1] That is a lesson that any company wishing to achieve long-term greatness needs to heed! Reinspire yourself or face superannuation!

[1] Darwin, Charles Gatton, *The Next Million Years*. Doubleday, 1953.

Select Bibliography

Bennett, S. Stewart III, and Stern, Joel M. *The Quest for Value: The EVA Management Guide*. Harper Business, 1987.

Bleeke, Joel and Ernst, David 'Is Your Strategic Alliance Really a Sale?' *Harvard Business Review*, July/August 1994.

Borg, Marcus *Jesus: A New Vision*. Harper and Row, 1988.

Bower, Joseph L. and Christensen, Clayton M. 'Disruptive Technologies: Catching the Waves'. *Harvard Business Review*, January/February 1995.

Boxwell, Robert J. *Benchmarking for Competitive Advantage*. McGraw-Hill, 1994.

Buzell, Robert D. and Gale, Bradley T. *The PIMS Principles: Linking Strategy to Performance*. The Free Press, 1987.

Camp, Robert C. *Benchmarking: The Search for Industry Best Practices that Lead to Superior Performance*. Quality Press, 1989.

Campbell, Andrew, Goold, Michael and Alexander, Marcus *Corporate Level Strategy: Creating Value in the Multi-Business Company*. John Wiley and Sons, 1994.

Champy, James *Reengineering Management: The Mandate for New Leadership*. Harper Business, 1995.

Clausewitz, Carl Von *On War*. Penguin, 1983.

Cooper, Robert G. *Winning at New Products: Accelerating the Process for Idea to Launch*. Addison-Wesley, 1993.

Copeland, Tom and Koller, Tim *Valuation: Measuring and Managing the Value of Companies*. 2nd edition. John Wiley and Sons, 1994.

Cragg, Kenneth *The House of Islam*. Wadsworth, 1988.

Danner, Victor *The Islamic Tradition*. Amity House, 1988.

Darwin, Charles Gatton *The Next Million Years*. Doubleday, 1953.

Davenport, Thomas H. and Prusak, Laurence *Working Knowledge. How Organisations Manage What They Know*. HBS Press, 1998.

Davidson, Bill and Davis, Stan *2020 Vision: Transforming Your Business Today To Succeed Tomorrow*. Simon and Schuster, 1991.

Davis, Stan *Future Perfect*. Addison-Wesley, 1987.

De Geus, Arie *The Living Company: Growth, Learning and Longevity in Business*. Nicholas Brealey Publishing, 1997.

Deming, W. Edwards *Quality, Productivity and Competitive Position*. MIT, 1982.

Edman, Irwin *Philosopher's Quest*. Doubleday, 1957.

Freemantle, David *What Customers Like About You: Adding Emotional Value for Service Excellence and Competitive Advantage*. Nicholas Brealey Publishing, 1998.

Fritzjof, Schuon *Understanding Islam*. Penguin, 1972.

Fuld, Leonard M. *Monitoring the Competition: Find Out What's Really Going On Over There*. John Wiley and Sons, 1998.

Ghoshal, Sumantra and Bartlett, Christopher A. *The Individualised Corporation: Great Companies are Defined by Purpose, Process and People*. Heinemann, 1998.

Gilad, Benjamin *Business Blind Spots: Replacing Your Company's Entrenched and Outdated Myths, Beliefs and Assumptions with Today's Reality*. Probus, 1994.

Goleman, Daniel *Emotional Intelligence*. 1995

Hamel, Gary and Prahalad, C.K. 'Competing for the Future'. *Harvard Business Review*, August 1984.

Hamel, Gary and Prahalad, C.K. *Competing for the Future: Breakthrough Strategies fore Seizing Control*. Harvard Business School Press, 1994.

Hammer, Michael *Beyond Reengineering*. Harper Business, 1995.

Hammer, Michael and Champy, James *Reengineering the Corporation: A Manifesto for Business Revolution*. Harper Business, 1994.

Hampden-Turner, Charles *Creating Corporate Culture: From Discord to Harmony*. Addison-Wesley, 1992.

Handy, Charles *Understanding Organizations*. Penguin, 1976.

Handy, Charles *The Empty Raincoat: Making Sense of the Future*. Arrow, 1995.

Hart, Christopher W.L. 'The Power of Unconditional Service Guarantees'. *Harvard Business Review*, October 1988.

Henderson, Bruce.D. *Henderson on Corporate Strategy*. New American Library, 1982.

Heskett, James L., Jones, Thomas O., Loveman, Gary, Sasser Junior, W. Earl and Schlesinger, Leonard A. 'Putting the Service Profit Chain to Work'. *Harvard Business Review*, March/April 1994.

Heskett, James L., Sasser, Earl and Hart, Christopher W.L. *Service Breakthroughs: Changing the Rules of the Game*. The Free Press, 1990.

Hobbes, Thomas *The Leviathan*. Penguin, 1986.

Imai, Masaaki *Kaizen*. Random House, 1986.

James, William *The Varieties of Religious Experience*. Macmillan, 1961.

Kanter, Rosabeth M. 'Collaborative Advantage: the Art of Alliances'. *Harvard Business Review*, July/August 1994.

Kaplan, Robert S. and Norton, David P. 'Putting the Balanced Scorecard to Work'. *Harvard Business Review*, September/October 1993.

Kaplan, Robert S. and Norton, David P. *The Balanced Scorecard: Translating Strategy into Action*. HBS Press, 1996.

Kapleau, Philip *The Three Pillars of Zen*. Anchor, 1989.

Katzenbach, Jon and Smith, Douglas *The Wisdom of Teams*. Harvard Business School Press, 1993.

Kinsley, David *Hinduism: A Cultural Perspective*. Prentice Hall, 1982.

Koch, Richard *Moses on Leadership: Or Why Everyone is a Leader*. Capstone, 1999.

Kohn, Alfie 'Why Incentive Plans Cannot Work'. *Harvard Business Review*, September/October 1993.

Kotler, Philip 'From Mass Marketing to Mass Customization'. *Planning Review*, September/October 1989.

Kotter, John and Heskett, James *Corporate Culture and Performance*. The Free Press, 1992.

Kotter, John P. 'Leading Change: Why Transformation Efforts Fail'. *Harvard Business Review*, March/April 1995.

Larkin, T.J. *Communicating Change*. McGraw-Hill, 1994.

Maister, David *Managing the Professional Service Firm*. Free Press, 1997.

McKenna, Regis *Real Time: Preparing for the Age of the Never Satisfied Customer*. HBS Press, 1997.

Merton, Thomas *The Way to Chuang Tzu*. New Directions, 1965.

Meyer, Christopher *Fast Cycle Time: How to Align Purpose, Strategy and Structure for Speed*. The Free Press, 1993.

Meyer, Christopher 'How the Right Measures Help Teams Excel'. *Harvard Business Review*, May/June 1994.

Milligan, Abraham *Jewish Worship*. Jewish Publication Society, 1971.

Mitchell, Stephen *Tao Te Ching*. Harper and Row, 1989.

Mohrman, Susan Albers, Cohen, Susan G. and Mohrman, Allan M. *Designing Team-Based Organizations: New Forms of Knowledge Work*. Jossey-Bass, 1995.

Moore, James. F. *The Death of Competition: Leadership and Strategy in the Age of Business Ecosystems.* John Wiley and Sons, 1996.

Myers, Paul. S. *Knowledge Management and Organizational Design.* Butterworth-Heinemann, 1996.

Negroponte, Nicholas *Being Digital: The Road Map for Survival on the Information Superhighway.* Hodder and Stoughton, 1995.

Ness, John B. *Man's Religions.* Macmillan, 1984.

Nonaka, Ikujiro and Takeushi, Hirotaka *The Knowledge Creating Company: How Japanese Companies Create the Dynamics of Innovation.* Oxford University Press, 1995.

Olins, Wally *Corporate Identity: Making Business Strategy Visible through Design.* Thames and Hudson, 1994.

Ostroff, Frank and Smith, Douglas 'The Horizontal Organization: Redesigning the Corporation'. *The McKinsey Quarterly*, No. 1, 1992.

Peppers, Don and Rogers, Martha *The One to One Future: Building Relationships One at a Time.* Currency Doubleday, 1993.

Peppers, Don and Rogers, Martha 'A New Marketing Paradigm: Share of Customer not Market Share'. *Planning Review*, March/April 1995.

Pickthall, Mohammed *The Meaning of the Glorious Koran.* New American Library, 1953.

Peters, Tom and Waterman, Robert *In Search of Excellence.* Warner Books, 1988.

Pine. B. Joseph, II *Mass Customization.* Harvard Business School Press, 1992.

Pine, B., Joseph, II, Peppers, Don and Rogers, Martha 'Do You Want to Keep Your Customers for Ever?' *Harvard Business Review*, March/April 1995.

Porass, Jerry J. and Collins, James C. *Built to Last: Successful Habits of Visionary Companies.* Harper Business, 1994.

Porter, Michael E. *Competitive Strategy. Techniques for Analyzing Industries and Competitors.* The Free Press, 1980.

Porter, Michael E. *Competitive Advantage: Creating and Sustaining Superior Performance.* The Free Press, 1985.

Porter, Michael E. 'From Competitive Advantage to Corporate Strategy'. *Harvard Business Review*, March 1987.

Porter, Michael E. *The Competitive Advantage of Nations.* The Free Press, 1993.

Poynter, Thomas A. and White, Roderick E. 'Making the Horizontal Organization Work'. *Business Quarterly*, Winter 1990.

Prahalad, C.K. and Hamel, Gary 'The Core Competencies of The Corporation'. *Harvard Business Review*, May/June 1990.

Pratt, J.B. *The Pilgrimage of Buddhism and a Buddhist Pilgrimage.* AMS Press, 1928.

Proust, Marcel *Remembrance of Things Past.* Random House, 1982.

Rappaport, Alfred *Creating Shareholder Value: A New Standard for Business.* The Free Press, 1986.

Ray, Darrell W. and Bronstein, Howard *Teaming Up: Making the Transition to a Self Directed, Team-based Organization.* McGraw-Hill, 1995.

Reichheld, Frederick F. 'Loyalty Based Management'. *Harvard Business Review*, March/April 1993.

Richman, Theodore and Koontz, Charles 'How Benchmarking Can Improve Business Reengineering'. *Planning Review*, December 1993.

Risher, Howard and Fay, Charles *The Performance Imperative: Strategies for Enhancing Workforce Effectiveness.* Jossey-Bass, 1995.

Robinson, Richard and Johnston, Will *The Buddhist Religion.* Wadsworth, 1982.

Ruggles, Rudy L. *Knowledge Management Tools.* Butterworth Heinemann, 1997.

Sammon, William L., Kurland, Mark A. and Spitalnic, Robert *Business Competitor Intelligence: Methods for Collecting, Organizing, and Using Information*. John Wiley and Sons, 1984.

Sawyer, Ralph D. *The Art of the Warrior: Leadership and Strategy from the Chinese Classics*. Shambhala Publications, 1996.

Schlesinger, Leonard A. and Heskett, James L. 'The Service-Driven Service Company'. *Harvard Business Review*, September/October 1991.

Scott, Mark C. *Value Drivers: The Manager's Guide to Driving Corporate Value Creation*. John Wiley and Sons, 1999.

Scott, Mark C. *The Intellect Industry: Profiting and Learning from Professional Services Firms*. John Wiley and Sons, 1998.

Schumacher, E.F. *A Guide for the Perplexed*. Harper and Row, 1976.

Seltzer, Robert M. *Jewish People, Jewish Thought*. Macmillan, 1980.

Smith, Huston *The World's Religions*. HarperCollins, 1991.

Spector, Robert A. *Taking Charge and Letting Go: Breakthrough Strategies for Creating and Managing the Horizontal Company*. The Free Press, 1995.

Stalk, George, Evans, Philip and Schulman, Lawrence E. 'Competing on Capabilities: The new Rules of Corporate Strategy'. *Harvard Business Review*, March/April 1992.

Stewart, Thomas A. *Intellectual Capital: The New Wealth of Organisations*. Nicholas Brealey Publishing, 1997.

Sveiby, Karl Erik *The New Organizational Wealth, Managing and Measuring Knowledge Based Assets*. Berrett-Koehler, 1997.

Thompson, Laurence G. *Chinese Religion*. Wadsworth, 1989.

Tomasko, Robert *Downsizing: Reshaping the Corporation for the Future*. 1987.

Waley, Arthur *The Way and Its Power*. Allen and Unwin, 1958.

Wellins, Richard S., Byham, William C. and Dixon, George R. *Inside Teams: How 20 World Class Organizations are Winning Through Teamwork*. Jossey-Bass, 1994.

Wheelwright, Steven C. and Clark, Kim *The Product Development Challenge: Competing Through Speed, Quality and Creativity*. Harvard Business School Press, 1995.

Zimmer, Heinrich *The Philosophies of India*. Princeton University Press, 1969.

Index

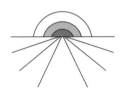